The Happiness Guide for Early Childhood Educators

*Secrets to Living Your Best Life
In and Out of the Classroom*

Brian Duprey
Kris Murray

Published by The Child Care Success Company

PO Box 3107
Crested Butte, CO 81224

www.childcaresuccess.com

Copyright© 2019 by Brian Duprey and Kris Murray

First edition 2019
Printed in the United States of America

This book is presented to:

_____

From:

_____

"If only you could sense how important you are to the lives of those you meet; how important you can be to people you may never even dream of. There is something of yourself that you leave at every meeting with another person."

~ Fred Rogers (Mr. Rogers)

"A hundred years from now it will not matter what my bank account was, the sort of house I lived in, or the kind of car I drove... but the world may be different because I was important in the life of a child."

~ Forest E. Witcraft

About the Authors

Kris Murray

Kris Murray is the President and Founder of The Child Care Success Company. She began the company in 2008 when the economy was starting to tank and the enrollment of her children's preschool was down significantly. They were about half full, desperate, and in need of answers. Taking her marketing knowledge and combining it with her "mom hat" she was able to create a system for her very first client (TLC Academy in Hudson, Ohio) that worked to grow their enrollment by about 55 children in 11 months. Together, they doubled their enrollment by putting proven but little-known marketing strategies into place. Today, they remain nearly full and have a waiting list for some rooms.

Kris took that success story and ran with it, turning it into a marketing system and toolkit for the child care business owner. Spreading the word through speaking engagements at state and national child care conferences, as well as online media and training webinars for partners and associations in the early childhood field, Kris began being sought out by child care owners. She made a commitment to dedicate the rest of her professional life to helping as many child care business owners, directors, and managers as she can with their enrollment, revenue, staff issues, time management, goal-setting, mindset, systems, and more. The biggest driver for Kris is when she is able to provide her clients with massive insight or clarity on how to fix a business challenge and they are inspired to take action to get results.

Kris believes that the child care industry is too high-risk and high-stress for it's workers to not be compensated well for the work that they do. She believes in transforming the minds of child care owners to have a positive mindset and live with daily gratitude, rather than having a fear-based approach. Mindset is the key ingredient to running a healthy, successful business. She is determined to help child care owners start leading happier, less stressful lives, and help them create an opportunity to make a good living through the amazing work that they do.

Always seeking to *"sharpen her saw,"* Kris became a John Maxwell Certified Coach in August 2019. Kris uses her Maxwell training to develop leadership capabilities in others. She is also certified in DISC Assessment and Training.

Born and raised in Cleveland, Ohio, Kris now resides in the mountains of Colorado with her two children, Owen and Maeve, and their rescued Labrador retriever, Simba. Kris loves all the outdoor activities Colorado has to offer (her favorite sport being downhill skiing) and enjoys taking time to travel to cross destinations off of her bucket list.

Kris Murray is also the author of three books that have helped thousands of owners and leaders become more effective with their marketing and enrollment-building. *The Ultimate Child Care Marketing Guide*, The *77 Best Strategies to Grow Your Early Childhood Program*, and *Rock Star Stories* are all available on Amazon.

Kris has been featured in Entrepreneur Magazine, INC Magazine, Newsweek, USA Today, Child Care Exchange, PBS Radio, and is proud to receive the Moving America Forward Award in 2016 for the impact she has made on the industry.

Brian Duprey

Brian Duprey is a seasoned 20-year veteran in the child care industry and a certified John Maxwell Business Coach. Before he and his wife, Carol, dove into the child care industry, Brian served in the United States Navy for eight years and later served five terms in the Maine Legislature as a State Representative, focusing on children's issues. Today, Brian and his wife have opened and operated nine different child care centers in central Maine.

In 2015 Brian attended his first Child Care Success Summit and immediately signed up to be a member of the Child Care Success Academy. Within two years of being a part of the CCSA, with Kris as his coach, Brian was able to double his revenues. Since being asked to join Kris Murray's team, Brian has continuously strived to help child care owners turn their hopes and dreams into realities and get out of overwhelm. He wants to see owners tackle the challenges that come with over-regulation in the industry and ensure that we carry out our mission of positively impacting over one million children.

Brian is the author of *Child Care Millionaire*, and it has been published as a part of the Kris Murray Library. This book is written for early childhood business owners wanting to grow their business into a (multi) million-dollar company: anyone from the home daycare provider that dreams of one day opening a center, to the small center owner who dreams of having a larger center, or a single center owner that wishes to have multiple centers. Brian shares 101 nuggets to bring your business to greater success. The book is available for purchase on Amazon.

Brian and his wife, Carol, have five children together, two of whom are involved in helping to run the business. When he isn't spending time with his children or busy being a grandpa to five grandchildren, Brian loves being on the water spending time sailing, fishing, boating, and scuba diving.

Kris and Brian have teamed up together to present to you this book, *The Happiness Guide for Early Childhood Educators*.

In today's world, it is very hard to find good teachers and even harder to keep them. Having well-rounded, happy teachers with a positive mindset is key to long-term retention of quality staff.

If you are an owner or director, please give a copy to all of your staff members and give a copy as part of your new hire onboarding process. Write a personal note in the book to make the teacher feel special, because they are!

Throughout this book, the use of she or her is used when referring to a teacher, director or owner. Whenever this is used, it should be understood as referring to both genders, unless specifically stated. This is done solely for the purpose of making the text easier to read, and no offense or sexism is intended.

Introduction

This book is made up of 99 gems. When you think of a gem, think of a diamond and how it was formed. A diamond was a piece of carbon that withstood a lot of time and pressure to form a beautiful gem. As a child care professional, you will have to withstand time and pressure as well. If you incorporate the gems in this book, your life will be so much more fulfilling and your impact on humanity will be much greater.

At the end of this book we have included profiles from early childhood professionals. Some are teachers, some are owners, some work outside the profession and serve the industry. The common thread that binds them all is they live the gems in this book each and every day.

There are many places in this book where we ask you to write things down. **PLEASE DO IT!** Please highlight, take notes and write in this book. You will get so much more out of it if you do that.

If you purchased this book on your own, ask your owner or leader to write a message in front of the book just for you. That way as you reflect back you can remember how much you are appreciated. Please enjoy the book, and remember that no one can make you have a bad day or a good day. How you live each day is entirely up to you.

~ Kris & Brian

Acknowledgements

We would like to thank all of the team members of the Child Care Success Company for the assistance and encouragement in helping us to get this book published.

To Sindye Alexander, thank you for your tireless dedication to oversee this project, you are a true child care rockstar.

To Katheryn Fisher, thank you for working so hard to format this book.

To Aubrey Knorr, thank you for working so diligently at editing and proofreading of this book.

And lastly to you, as the reader of this book, thank you for taking the first step to having a much happier life.

Enjoy!

Table of Contents

Early Childhood Educator Profiles:

Preface

More than likely you fall into one of four different categories, or possibly multiple categories (owner/director).

1. **Owner**
2. **Management (Director/Assistant Director)**
3. **Teacher**
4. **Support Staff   (Aides, Driver, Maintenance, Cook, etc.)**

Each one of you will take something different out of this book, but reading every gem is very important. You may not think that a gem is applicable to you but it is important to read each and every one of them because it is important to understand everyone's role within the company.

Child Care Owner

As an owner, you have, by far, the most stressful job in the company. Decisions you make affect everyone in the company from the employees who work for you to the parents who trust you to watch their children. More than likely, you have invested considerable sums of money into your center(s) and have put everything you own at risk to provide an amazing early childhood education to children of strangers.

You deserve a pat on the back and we are here to give it to you. Being a child care center owner is quite possibly one of the loneliest jobs in the world. We equate it to being on an island all by yourself. Some days no one likes you, including your staff, your customers, and even the kids you care for. It is not like you can call the center owner down the road and bounce ideas off her and talk about your struggles: she is a competitor.

We have an amazing mastermind group for center owners

that have a licensed capacity of 49 or greater and some of the centers in our group have up to 28 locations. It is a high-end mastermind group where we provide professional coaching, guidance, and networking unsurpassed in our industry.

If you are an owner of a center licensed for 49 or more children, are tired of feeling so alone, and want hundreds of other child care owners as a support system, please visit www.childcaresuccess.com. Sign up for a free strategy session coaching call with a member of our coaching team. We will see if you are the right fit to be in our mastermind group.

We would love to meet you! We both speak each year at the Child Care Success Summit™ in early fall. If you attend, please bring this book with you and one of us will personalize it for you. This event is the world's largest conference on the business side of child care. For information and tickets please visit www.childcaresuccesssummit.com.

Child Care Director/Assistant Director

If an owner has hired you to be a director or assistant director, congratulations! You have one of the most important positions in the company and are trusted with a huge responsibility. More than likely you will handle finances, you will deal with employee problems, you will have parents yelling at you, and you will have to make difficult decisions on whether a child was abused. You may do all of the above by lunch on Monday!

Now that you know that we think you are amazing, it is time to tell yourself that. We have come across hundreds of directors and assistant directors in our careers as child care coaches and we see a general theme in many of them - they lack leadership skills and struggle with mindset issues.

If you struggle to lead a team of employees, this book is for you. If you look in the mirror and do not see the most amazing person in the world staring back at you, then this book is for you.

We would like you to read this book, take notes, and start

practicing the gems that are in the book; they are truly life-changing. Let them change your life and then do us a favor: get a copy of this book for every one of your team members. Write a personal note to your team member on page iii, and let them know how special they are. It would mean the world to them and this book will change their life.

Child Care Teacher/Assistant Teacher

If you are a teacher of young children you are one of the most special people on the planet. The love and patience we see exhibited by the teachers we have met in the field have been remarkable.

We both have seen many of the struggles teachers have faced throughout the years as well. Many teachers struggle with issues like self-image, self-care, positive mindset, relationships, addiction, personal finances, work ethic, and more.

We have written this book to help you. If you take each gem very seriously and apply it to your daily life you will see miraculous things start happening. You will feel more refreshed, you will be empowered in making decisions, and you will be able to look in the mirror and love the person staring back at you.

If you have bought this book on your own, please take this book to your owner and director and have them write a positive saying to you on page iii. If this book was a gift from your owner or director the way to show them thanks is to read this book in its entirety and start living your best life.

There are 99 gems in this book divided into seven chapters. You may not think the leadership chapter applies to you, but it does. You lead children, you lead the parents of the children, and you will lead your director (this will be explained in the gem about leading-up).

If you enjoy the book, please recommend it to others in our industry. There are a lot of teachers that need many of the gems in this book. Thank you, in advance, for helping us to reach them, as it is our mission in life to make a difference in as many lives as we possibly can. Thank you for allowing us a chance to change your life for the better.

Support Staff (Aide, Receptionist, Maintenance, Cook, etc.)

You may be thinking "Why would I need to read *The Happiness Guide for Early Childhood Educators*?" Why did someone give me this book to read?" You were given this book for one reason; someone cares deeply about you.

In this book are 99 gems full of information on living your best life, which many people fail to do each day. If you trust the person who gave you this book and read and apply each gem into your daily routine, your life will change for the better, we promise you that!

Thank you for what you do to support the entire staff, your jobs are very important. Without a cook, the children would go hungry. Without the maintenance person the lights may not shine. Each support person has a vital role in running an effective center and is an equally important part of the team.

You may think the engine is the most important part of the train, but what happens if the wheels break on the second car? All team members carry equal weight, but on the other hand, a chain is only as strong as its weakest link. If there is a weak link in the child care center team, everyone suffers. This is why you were given this book: you are a valued member of the team and the team cannot afford to *not* have you living your best life. Enjoy the book and thank you again for what you do to improve the lives of children.

A Tale of Two Teachers:

Teresa and Jillian

Teresa Moore and Jillian Jones are a team of two Pre-K teachers at Leapfrog Preschool, based in a suburb of Atlanta. Teresa is the lead teacher, has been at this school for seven years, and has 15 years of early childhood experience. She has a Bachelor's degree in ECE and is thinking about going back to get her Master's Degree. Jillian is fairly new to the early learning field, with 2 years of experience. Teresa is 38 years old and Jillian is 24.

Before being transferred to the Pre-K room to work with Teresa, Jillian worked with toddlers in Ms. Susan's room. She showed promise as a teacher but it became clear fairly quickly that Jillian would be more effective with the four year old children rather than toddlers. Her desire & ability to embrace kindergarten readiness assessments and the Pre-K curriculum components were two things that her director observed. Jillian also lacked patience in the toddler room and struggled to stay calm and loving with the younger children.

Teresa and Jillian's director, Donna, wanted her team to get some professional development in the areas of mindset, teamwork, relationships, and communication, so they could become a stronger unified team and work together better in each classroom setting. They currently read books together in a monthly professional development book club, listen to audiobooks and podcasts, and watch YouTube training videos designed to help in each of these areas. Donna also brings in guest speakers from time to time to do special training sessions.

As a result, Teresa and Jillian are starting to experience the impact of ongoing personal growth, both as individuals and together as a teacher team. We will follow their journey throughout this book.

Chapter 1

Making a Difference

"Never underestimate the valuable and important difference you make in every life you touch, for the impact you make today has a powerful rippling effect on every tomorrow."

~ Leon Brown

A child will learn more in a four year child care program that he or she would ever learn from four years in college. The brain in the first five years of development will make more neurological connections than it will make in the rest of that person's entire life.

How is that for making a difference? You are laying the foundation for that child to excel in life. You are a teacher! You make a difference!

There is no other profession that will allow you to make such an incredible difference in the lives of so many people, like child care, and that impact will be felt for generations like a ripple across a pond on a quiet day.

This chapter is made up of seven very important gems that help you to solidify what motivates you and why you are doing what you are doing.

So be proud of what you do each day, you are not a babysitter, you are a part of a team of difference-makers. Go forth and change the world, one child at a time.

Gem #1

Write Down Your *"Why"*

"There is no greater gift you can give or receive than to honor your calling. It's why you were born. And how you become most truly alive."

~ Oprah Winfrey

What makes you get out of bed in the morning motivated to spend the day teaching another person's child? Why do you go to the store and buy supplies for your classroom with your own money? Where does the force come from that causes you to lose sleep when one of the children in your care is suffering in some way?

Why do you do it? We are sure you have been asked this question before. Is it your calling? Is it just a job, or do you consider it your profession? Do you have fun doing it? Do you feel you are making a difference in the life of a child? Is this your ministry?

> *What makes you get out of bed in the morning motivated to spend the day teaching another person's child?*

Answering these questions helps to answer the fundamental question of why you do what you do. Until you know exactly WHY you do what you do, you will never truly be able to give your very best each and every day.

You see, your *"why"* is your fuel. What happens to a car when you run out of fuel? It ceases to run. When you run out of the reasons why you do what you do, you will quickly spiral into becoming a liability instead of an asset to your fellow team members and will no longer be an effective teacher.

Please put this book down and take 10-15 minutes to ponder why you do what you do in early childhood education. After you come up with the top 3-5 reasons, we would like you to write them below.

1. _____

2. _____

3. _____

4. _____

5. _____

We would like you to either type these and print them out, or write them out on paper and place them on your refrigerator at home. This is very important, so please do not skip this step. If you are worried about what other people think, then place them on your wall in your bedroom. Just place them somewhere that you can look at them each and every day.

Why is it important to look at this list every day? Having a positive reminder of why you do what you do will allow you to carry on in the face of adversity. You will have a bad day, we all do. You will want to quit, we all do. You will feel like a failure, we all do.

Once you have a why firmly entrenched into your subconscious mind, nothing will be able to get you down. A bad day will not derail you. You will not want to quit when the going gets tough. You will not want to quit your job making a difference to go work in fast food for $1.00 more an hour because your why is so much more important than a slightly larger paycheck.

Remember this important gem on making a difference: **Write down your "*why*."**

Teresa & Jillian's Story

After reading this gem, Teresa and Jillian wrote down their "*why's*" and shared them with each other. Teresa knew she wanted to work with children ever since she was a little girl. She had a babysitting service as a teenager, and she became known as the best, most reliable babysitter in her neighborhood by the time she was 15. When she graduated from high school, she knew she wanted to get a degree in early childhood.

Teresa's passion is brain development and helping kids learn. She loves the "*light bulb moment*" when a child has an insight through discovery and trial & error. After reading this gem, Teresa instantly knew that her "*why*" was using her early learning expertise in experiential learning to help children have that "*light bulb*" moment, and develop a lifelong love of learning.

On the other hand, Jillian wasn't so sure of her "*why*," so she gave it a few days of hard thinking and reflection. Later that week, on a field trip with her Pre-K students, Jillian realized that she loved getting out of the center with her kids and taking adventures. She had such a good time on the field trip to the outdoor nature center, and she conveyed to the kids in a super-engaging way that they were "*on an adventure together.*" This day was probably her favorite in her new career so far. She decided to state her "*why*" as a passion for revealing new adventures to children and helping them craft those adventures into learning experiences. She shared with Teresa her insights around this idea, and the two of them (with Donna's input) started planning a quarterly field trip calendar as well as weekly onsite "*adventures*" that Teresa could lead with the children on the school grounds.

This created a high level of job fulfillment for Teresa and especially for Jillian, as they gained clarity about their "*whys*" and strategically grew the opportunities to capitalize on them and improve the learning experience for the children in their classroom.

Gem #2

Early Childhood Education is the Most Impactful Profession

"An investment in knowledge pays the best dividends."

~ Benjamin Franklin

No other profession on Earth has a greater impact on humanity than early childhood education. Whether you are a teacher, a director or a center owner, what you do has a greater impact on the planet than being a doctor, lawyer, rocket scientist, or even a military member.

> *No other profession on Earth has a greater impact on humanity than early childhood education.*

You have the most important job in the world, why do you not treat it that way? Are you embarrassed to tell people what you do for fear of being judged? You are not a babysitter; you are a difference-maker.

A child will learn more by the age of five than he or she will learn the rest of their lives. A teacher at a child care center will teach a child more things that are retained than any college professor ever will when that child reaches college age.

Stop selling yourself short. Take some pride in what you do. You are making a difference in the lives of future doctors, lawyers, rocket scientists, and military personnel. So when someone asks what you do, the answer is, *"I am a difference-maker,"* because that is what you are.

Remember this important gem on making a difference: **Early childhood education is the most impactful**

profession.

Gem #3

Every Child is Special

"We worry about what a child will become tomorrow, yet we forget that he is someone today."

~ Stacia Tauscher

One day Thomas Edison came home and gave a paper to his mother. He told her, *"My teacher gave this paper to me and told me to only give it to my mother."*

His mother's eyes were tearful as she read the letter out loud to her child: Your son is a genius. This school is too small for him and doesn't have enough good teachers for training him. Please teach him yourself.

> *We all have that one child that steps on your very last nerve and tests the very fiber of your patience each and every day.*

One day, many years after Edison's mother died and he was now one of the greatest inventors of the century, he was looking through old family things. Suddenly he saw a folded paper in the corner of a drawer in a desk. He took it and opened it up. On the paper was written: Your son is addled [mentally ill]. We won't let him come to school anymore.

Edison cried for hours and then he wrote in his diary: *"Thomas Alva Edison was an addled child that, by a hero mother, became the genius of the century."* Thomas Edison – Interview.

We all have that one child that steps on your very last nerve and tests the very fiber of your patience each and every day. We have heard many stories in our careers in the industry and most of them have a common theme, the child's home life has been turned upside down.

In today's world, many children are growing up without two loving parents to provide stability and security to the child. We have seen single moms bring a different man into their child's world every 3-4 months, causing the child to have separation problems as they become attached to different fatherly figures.

We have seen children of divorce who are spending half of their time with mom and a new man and the other half with dad and a new woman. Normally in these instances of new love, the children feel left out and abandoned and develop a lack of security thinking they are next to go.

Before we start getting hate mail, we are not saying that a single mom cannot raise a child. We are also not saying that a same-sex couple cannot raise a child. We have seen both done very successfully. What we are saying is that children need loving parents and stability. The more instability in a child's life, the more chance for that child to act out.

As a child care professional, you need to be aware of the child's home life to best know how to teach the child. Acting up at school is normally an outward display of internal feelings that are normally a cry for help or attention. Every child is special, Thomas Edison's mom thought so. Had it not been for her giving him love and attention, the world would have been robbed of a brilliant mind.

When you are faced with a child that has you ready to pull your hair out, please think of the story of Thomas Edison and realize that the child who is causing you problems today may cure cancer 30 years from now. Refer to your list of why's that were created in gem#1. Maybe then you will have a little more patience for a child with a home life that he or she did not ask for.

Remember this important gem on making a difference:

Every child is special.

Teresa & Jillian's Story

In teacher training, both Jillian and Teresa have been repeatedly taught that each child is an individual, has huge potential, and retains an "*imprint*" of key humans that they spend time within their first six years of life. They know their words and actions toward each child are crucially important.

In practice, however, this can be easier said than done. Imagine a sometimes chaotic classroom with challenging behavior shown by a few students in particular. It can be extremely difficult for Teresa and Jillian to actually remember that every child is special and has unique gifts to share with the world in these times of stress and chaos.

To practice kindness, gentleness, patience, and positive, encouraging communication with each child in these types of situations is indeed a gift that preschool teachers bring to the party like no one else.

So this gem was a great reminder for both teachers, that every child is special. They were inspired to take this gem to the next level the next time they were able to go to lunch together (which is rare, since one is usually covering the other one).

During nap time, a great floater teacher named Cindy popped in for an hour to cover them so they could go to lunch together. At lunch, Jillian and Teresa wrote down every child's name in their classroom, and a few sentences about what makes that child special, at this point in their development. They had some great laughs, a few tears, and made a "*teacher team plan*" to work on developing the special-ness of each child in their care.

This, in turn, made them more engaged teachers, as they worked together more deeply to impact children in their classroom, and caught smiles to each other across the room throughout the day.

Gem #4

Leave a Legacy

"All good men and women must take responsibility to create legacies that will take the next generation to a level we could only imagine."

~ Jim Rohn

Have you ever thought of your profession as one that leaves a legacy? The year that you spend with a child leaves an indelible impression on their brain that they will have for the rest of their lives. A piece of you has been left in their minds; this is your legacy.

Come to work each day excited to leave a legacy so when you are gone, a big piece of you will live on in the lives of others.

No matter what that child accomplishes in life, you deserve some of the credit. More than likely the child will not remember you later in life, just like you probably do not remember the doctor that delivered you into this world, yet it does not mean it is any less significant. You made a difference in this child's life in the year you have spent together and your legacy lives on as each child moves on.

Come to work each day excited to leave a legacy so when you are gone, a big piece of you will live on in the lives of others. If you live like this each and every day you will have truly lived a life of significance.

Remember this important gem on making a difference: **Leave a legacy.**

Gem #5

Teach the Children Continually

"Better than a thousand days of diligent study is one day with a great teacher."

~ Japanese Proverb

Most children are in a child care setting for 8 to 10 hours a day. Unfortunately, in many programs, there are only 2-3 hours of learning to happen in that timeframe. Why is this? Because many teachers think that unless you are sitting in front of the children teaching, they are not learning.

As a teacher, you must find creative ways for children to learn throughout the entire day. Many of the clients that we coach have set up outdoor classrooms with learning stations outside. What used to be free play outside has turned into outdoor education.

> *You are going to be far more valuable to the children than any college professor ever will be.*

Set up creative learning stations inside of your classroom so the children can explore and learn on their own. Ask a lot of questions of the children and spark their curiosity.

You do not have to physically teach the child the entire day, but you must find a way to expand their mind even when at play. A child's mind is like a sponge and is capable of learning every minute of every day. Make sure you have the tools necessary to help them and you will be making more of a difference than you will ever know. It all begins with the proper mindset. From this point forward consider yourself a professor of early childhood education, because that is what you are. You are going to be far more valuable to the children than any college professor ever will be.

Remember this important gem on making a difference: **Teach the children continually.**

Gem #6

Value Your Work

"Your beliefs become your thoughts,

Your thoughts become your words,

Your words become your actions,

Your actions become your habits,

Your habits become your values,

Your values become your destiny."

~Gandhi

If you traveled in a time machine and found out that one of the children in your care would grow up to be President of the United States, would you treat that child any different each and every day? The answer should be no, and let us tell you why.

> *The secret is to value each child as though they can be whatever they want to be in life because they can.*

In any given day you may cut up food for the first astronaut to step foot on Mars; you may help put the jacket on the first female Chief Justice of the Supreme Court; you may read to the child who one day grows up to discover the cure for cancer; or you may play silly games with a future cardiologist.

The secret is to value each child as though they can be whatever they want to be in life because they can. In most cases, you are only second to the child's parents as the most influential person in that child's life. You are the one that is giving him or her a love of learning, which is vital to make a difference in this world.

So the next time you think that what you are doing is mundane work, try picturing these little humans for what they really are; seeds of potential that can be whatever they want in life. Love them, nurture them, and allow them to soak up your knowledge and always instill in them the belief that all things are possible - because they are!

Remember this important gem on making a difference: **Value your work.**

Gem #7

T.E.A.M. Together Everyone Achieves More

"Alone we can do so little, together we can do so much."

~Helen Keller

All too often we get into our jobs as educators never having been part of a team before. For many early educators, this is the only job they have ever had. Working with others is something that does not come naturally. Just as children must learn to work together and learn to share, a team needs to learn to work together and learn to share.

We tend to think of the classroom as "*my*" classroom and think of the kids as "*my*" kids. While it's great for a teacher to take ownership, it is also important to work for the common good and work as a team - otherwise, the

> *A team member never gossips about another team member behind his or her back, ever.*

culture of your school will suffer.

In order for a team to be effective at working together, it must, at a minimum, adhere to a set of standards that are non-negotiable. Here is an example of some team principals; we encourage owners and directors to come up with a set for your center:

- A team member never gossips about another team member behind his or her back, ever.
- A team member always pulls his or her weight.
- A team member will always mentor new team members on how to better fit within the team.
- A team member will never talk badly about any team members, including management and owners as well as customers and children.
- A team member will do more than is expected of him or her.
- A team member is always honest.

Together everyone achieves more if you work as a team instead of acting as individuals. Centers that do the best job at making a difference are the ones that have a team that functions well together.

Remember this important gem on making a difference: **Together everyone achieves more.**

Teresa & Jillian's Story

As a team of two, running the Pre-K program, Teresa and Jillian thought they were a pretty good fit. They seemed to get along most of the time, helped each other on tough days, and each believed she contributed 100% to the success of their classroom.

One random Wednesday, Teresa seemed especially drained and low-energy, and after a couple of hours in the classroom, she began making sarcastic remarks toward Jillian. It seemed that everything Jillian said got twisted around in meaning to suit Teresa's snarky comments. Then Jillian found out from another teacher on her break that Teresa had been spreading some untrue gossip about her. Jillian was in tears, super upset, and went to seek out Donna for support and counsel.

Donna listened to Jillian and calmed her down. She assured her that the situation would get resolved because these two teachers had an otherwise positive, strong relationship. Donna later approached Teresa and asked her about the issue, in the privacy of Donna's office. Teresa then also broke down in tears and said that she had been having some rough nights with her husband and that her marriage was on the rocks. She admitted to taking it out on Jillian and even made up some false gossip in her weakest moment. Teresa felt horrible, and it felt great to talk it out with Donna and admit her mistakes.

The two women were then brought in to Donna's office together for a sharing and hugging session. They worked it out through *open and honest* dialogue. Jillian forgave Teresa and gained some compassion about her home life issues. Teresa found a marriage counselor and promised to attend with her husband, which they did, and things started to turn around.

The two teachers forged an even stronger partnership as team members in their Pre-K classroom. They became true TEAM members for one another and grew together as a team, rather than apart as siloed teachers pretending to like one another.

Chapter 1 Notes:

_____

_____

_____

_____

_____

_____

_____

_____

_____

_____

_____

_____

_____

_____

_____

_____

Chapter 2

Health & Wellness

"The best six doctors and no one can deny it; are sunshine, water, rest, air, exercise, and diet."

~ Wayne Fields

Why have we included a chapter on health and wellness in a child care mindset and leadership book? The answer is simple, our health and wellness are the keys to a positive mindset and effective leadership.

If you do not like what you see when you look in the mirror, how are you going to be able to have a positive mindset?

If you are drinking 10 cups of coffee each day and living on potato chips and doughnuts, how are you going to keep up with an active classroom of four year olds?

If you don't learn to relax, how are you going to be around long enough to see your own grandchildren graduate from college?

Life does not allow us a mulligan; we only get one shot. We need to make it count. Take this chapter and all of the gems we have given you like it's a chance to lengthen your life; increase your stamina and be excited when you look into the mirror.

We look forward to hearing all of the success stories of those who took this chapter seriously and changed their lives for the better.

Gem #8

Health is Vitally Important

"The greatest wealth is health."

~ Virgil

YOLO: You only live once. A great motto to live your life by, but all too often that motto is used for something that is not good for you. You want to order a large steak but instead choose a salad and the person you are with says, "*Hey, you only live once.*"

> *We need to ensure that we have a healthy mind, body, and spirit.*

Since we only get one bite at the apple, we need to make it count. Health is so much more than good eating habits, and we need to make smart decisions to ensure that we live long enough on our first and only shot at life.

We need to ensure that we have a healthy mind, body, and spirit. Proper eating habits produce a healthy body; proper mindset produces a healthy mind; also living a life of significance will yield a healthy spirit.

Like an infectious disease, these positive traits will infect others around you if you share with others the secret to your health, happiness and overall well-being. Since the majority of people you speak with on a daily basis may be overweight, unhappy, or negative, you will stick out like a sore thumb. Use this to your advantage to share with other people the importance of a healthy mind, body, and spirit, and you will be helping to make a difference in the lives of more than just children.

Remember this important gem on health and wellness: **Health is vitally important.**

Gem #9

Create Healthy Eating Habits

"Those who think they have no time for healthy eating...will sooner or later have to find time for illness."

~ Edward Stanley

We get it; fast food by its mere definition is more convenient to get on your short lunch hour. Our question to you is, why didn't you pack a healthy lunch the night before? It is far cheaper to buy your own food, make it at home, and bring it to work with you than to eat out. Doing so will allow you to make healthy choices.

> *Employees who eat well and exercise frequently call in sick less often.*

Some people benefit from eating fewer meals with more hours in between, and some people like to eat more frequent small meals. Whatever you prefer, shoot for at least HALF of each plate to be full of fruits and fresh veggies. If you pack chopped veggies or a salad to bring to lunch, you will feel much more energy than if you rely on fast food.

Drink lots of water. You should be drinking a gallon of water a day to stay hydrated and flush all the toxins out of your body. Coffee may have water in it but does not count because caffeine is a diuretic (which means it will dehydrate you). Be sure to drink lots of plain old water to help your body stay healthy.

You should drink two bottles of water right when you get up to jump-start your organs and flush out toxins. You should also drink a bottle of water before every meal and every two hours throughout the day, including right before bed.

Employees who eat well and exercise frequently call in sick less often. So eating poorly costs you money in more ways than one. When you go to a restaurant, be sure to look at the calories and limit your choices to whatever calorie goal you have set yourself for that day. It doesn't matter so much what you eat as long as you burn off as much as you take in.

Slow down when you are eating. The more you chew your food before swallowing the easier it will be to digest it, which will allow the body to burn it for fuel instead of storing it as fat. It should take you at least 20 minutes to finish a meal.

Eating while stressed has been proven to pack pounds onto your body. Try to get to a state of relaxation 5-10 minutes prior to eating and for up to 30 minutes after. Eating under stress causes the body's fight or flight response to trigger the release of chemicals in your body that will help to store fat. Relaxing before, during and after meals will burn fat instead of storing it.

For most people, 3500 calories are equal to one pound. This means that if you eat 500 calories a day more than you burn off you will gain a pound a week. Flip that around and if you burn 500 more calories a day more than you consume, you will lose a pound a week. This varies based on a person's metabolism, but it is a good rule of thumb.

We are not asking you to go on a diet; we are asking you to make a lifestyle change. Develop healthy eating habits, which will give you more stamina, help you to lose a few pounds, and will help you to feel better.

Remember this important gem on health and wellness: **Create healthy eating habits.**

Gem #10

Exercise at Work Each Day

"Life is like riding a bicycle. To keep your balance, you must keep moving."

~ Albert Einstein

"I have no time to go to the gym." We are sure the vast majority of those of you reading this book will tell us this. Since the average person today spends 2-4 hours a day on his or her cell phone, don't tell us you do not have time to go to the gym.

So let's just say we buy your excuse that you do not have time. Maybe you are ambitious and work two jobs and truly do not have time; then you need to exercise at work.

Most child care center owners will allow you to exercise with the children. We have had many employees over the years that have done amazing cardio workouts with the children, both inside and out. The secret is

Most child care center owners will allow you to exercise with the children.

to always keep moving and to wear a device that tracks your steps. This way you can set goals and make sure you do not go to bed at night until you reach your step goal.

Talk to your director or owner about adding an exercise program into the children's routine, and involve as many staff members as possible. Plan inside and outside exercise time and let parents know that you are doing your part to keep the children healthy to lower childhood obesity rates.

Remember this important gem on health and wellness: **Exercise at work each day.**

Teresa & Jillian's Story

Like many early educators, Teresa and Jillian often struggle with putting themselves first. They work so hard taking care of the little ones in their classroom, they often don't have the energy or motivation to think about eating right, packing healthy lunches, or carving out time to exercise. Running around after four year olds often seems to be exercise enough!

However, their leader Donna has been trying to support all the staff with more health and wellness opportunities, including smoothie days, healthy snacks stocked in the break room, time outs to walk and stretch, and a new employee benefit - partially paid gym memberships.

Jillian decided to take advantage of this new benefit and spent $30 a month out of her own pocket, matched by Donna, to join a local gym. She even invested a few sessions to workout with a trainer, to give her a kick start. Jillian was measured prior to starting, and she was a little embarrassed to discover she had a body fat percentage of 37%, and she weighed 172 pounds.

After working out for a few months, she felt great, lost 5% body fat, lost a few pounds, and got considerably more toned. Most importantly, she felt stronger, had more energy for her job, and showed up happier and more positive in her mindset.

Teresa was inspired by her colleague and decided to start walking with weights every evening, as baby steps into fitness.

One year later, Jillian had dropped 10 pounds overall and replaced 20 pounds of fat on her frame with lean muscle. She looked great and everyone in her life took notice – especially her boyfriend, Daniel.

The most important point to share here is that no matter what you do in life – teacher, parent, spouse, friend – you cannot pour from an empty cup. You've got to protect yourself from getting depleted. You've got to watch your "*cup*" to make sure it stays close to full if not full. One of the best ways to do that is to work on improving your healthy habits, like eating lots of fruits and veggies, and making time in your day, week, and life to exercise.

Gem #11

Practice Meditation

"Meditation brings wisdom; lack of meditation leaves ignorance. Know well what leads you forward and holds you back, and choose the path that leads to wisdom."

~ Buddha

By Annie Kuehlhorn L.M.T, Doula and Wellness Coach

I did not start out as a meditator. I was curious about the practice because I kept hearing about those I admire using the practice of meditation consistently.

I'm here to help you, and myself, tap into our best selves – it's my life's mission which I've been working on in various roles for decades. As a doula and midwife's assistant, massage therapist, mother, wife, client care specialist, and other important roles – I've been learning the ways we can nurture our bodies, minds, hearts, and souls.

> *We can take care of our spirit by dancing, sharing moments with others, and doing absolutely nothing.*

We have so many strategies on how we can do this. For example, we can take care of our physical bodies with nutrition, exercise, and great sleep. We can take care of our minds with reading and learning. We can take care of our spirit by dancing, sharing moments with others, and doing absolutely nothing. In fact – doing absolutely nothing (aka meditating) can impact all aspects of our human experiences.

Meditation has scientifically proven benefits (I dare you, Google it!). 'Doing Nothing' can improve your body's health, increase your mental stabilities, level out your emotional waves, help create deeper and more meaningful bonds with yourself and the love you have for others.

I am a meditator because of the overall benefits I gain from this practice. And it's not filled with bald-headed dudes in robes nor weird rituals that are out of your comfort zone. It's literally about doing nothing, in a place and position you are comfortable in. It can be for one minute or longer too.

Here is a simple practice I use regularly and I offer it to you to try. Test this out like you might a jacket. Put it on, feel it. Alter it as you see fit. The goal here is for you to attempt 'doing nothing' three times in the next three days. Are you in? How might a daily practice benefit you?

Feel free to turn on some background music, monks chanting, classical, whatever sounds calming to you. A search on most any platform for meditation music will lead you to something you might enjoy. Turn off all other distractions.

Sit in a comfortable position (it does not have to be the traditional lotus position to start, let's just get you comfortable and in the habit!)

As the music plays in, take some deep breaths and simply notice your breath. Give thanks to the air you breathe, the way your lungs work, and feel your heart beating.

Imagine a ball of light and energy above the earth. Allow that ball of energy to bring light beams to the crown of your head. Allow that energy to float down through your face, to the back of your throat, to your heart and imagine it circling around your heart. Simply allow the energy to fill you. If thoughts come up, no problem, let them come up, observe and go back to the energy filling your entire being. Use a mantra, Sat Nam or Om are simple to use at first. When thoughts come in, smile at them, push them away and concentrate on your breath or mantra. Whatever you do – don't be a meditating perfectionist! Perfection is our lowest standard.

The mind is going to flow thoughts through it. We can enjoy the practice of doing nothing and notice those breaks between the thoughts. That's a bliss moment.

When your song ends, take a deep breath and thank yourself for allowing the rest of the world to happen while you tune your mind. As you get used to sitting in stillness you might find you crave meditating for longer. When I get off track on my daily practice I re-commit to five minutes a day and eventually I am up to 30 minutes a day as I enjoy the feeling in the moment and for the rest of the day. There is no right or wrong. It's a practice. A practice that will pay off as you instill the habit.

For me, my meditation practice has given me more peaceful moments in my day, helped me to clarify things, quiet my mind, and it is adding more love in my life.

I'm here following along my own path to wisdom, sometimes bumbling along and other times locking into the flow of life. Meditation is helping me lock more into the flow of life. And it brings me more insights into how I can help you tap into your best self.

You do the work. And I can support and nurture you along

the way. Often, after a couple of kids, mamas can feel stuck in their marriage, overwhelmed with parenting or lost in their career, I get that! I have created a 12-week program for women looking to get back into alignment with their highest self and energy through healthy habit change, coaching to get them more connected with their mind, body, and spirit. Visit www.akwellness.net for more information.

And until we cross paths again – please enjoy 'doing nothing' today. It's easy and relaxing, Sat Nam.

Remember this important gem on health and wellness: **Practice Meditation.**

Gem #12

Healthy Relationships Only

"A loving relationship is one in which the loved one is free to be himself — to laugh with me, but never at me; to cry with me, but never because of me; to love life, to love himself, to love being loved. Such a relationship is based upon freedom and can never grow in a jealous heart."

~ Leo F. Buscaglia

Many who enter the child care field do so because of a trauma in their childhood. For many, there was a lack of love in their upbringing which working with children and feeling that love each day makes up for.

If you have had trauma in your childhood, we are very sorry this has happened to you. There is no reason that you need to have further trauma in your life by getting into an unhealthy relationship.

We would describe an unhealthy relationship as one where there is abuse or neglect of one of the partners in the relationship. Most have a common theme, the employee had low self-esteem and attracted a partner who took advantage of them and did not treat them as the special person that they are.

You deserve to be treated with respect and dignity. In our chapter on mindset, we are going to help you to love yourself before you can love others. If you truly love yourself, you would never let yourself be treated poorly.

You deserve to be treated with respect and dignity.

If you are not in a relationship at this time, we are going to help you raise your standards so this would never happen to you. Read each gem in the Mindset chapter and incorporate them into your daily life; you will quickly feel more deserving of an amazing relationship and know that you deserve to be treated with the utmost dignity and respect.

Remember this important gem on health and wellness: **Healthy relationships only.**

Gem #13

Avoid Tobacco, Alcohol, and Drugs

"To keep the body in good health is a duty, otherwise we shall not be able to keep our mind strong and clear."

~ Buddha

Let us first talk about tobacco. Quit. Now! If you do not smoke, never start. With all we know today about the ill health effects of smoking, why on earth would anyone want to do it? Nothing bothers us more than to see a young person smoking today, especially someone who teaches children.

If you are a smoker, your children are much more likely to be smokers, which means you are shortening their lives by being a poor role model. It is never too late to quit; your body will begin healing itself within days.

Alcohol is a drug and a highly addictive drug. Something as simple as a drink or two a day can become a habit that becomes hard to break. Alcohol is a diuretic, which means you will become dehydrated with excessive alcohol use and not properly hydrating. When you are dehydrated, your vital organs do not work as designed and it stresses the body out. If you choose to drink socially, limit yourself to no more than one drink every 2-3 hours and drink lots of water. Doing so will make sure that you are properly hydrated, you are sober enough to make rational decisions, and you will be able to drive if needed. Drinking more than that can cause you to make very poor, life-altering choices that you can never take back.

Illegal drugs are the dumbest things a teacher can ever do.

A teacher choosing to use illegal drugs is showing poor judgment. If you need to take drugs to feel good, or to try to drown out a negative past, then you have a mindset problem. Read this book several times and every time you want to get high begin reading. We have written this book to help you start making changes in your life. Hopefully, if you are abusing tobacco, alcohol or drugs you will change your life starting today. Remember, you are a role model for the children that you care for.

Remember this important gem on health and wellness: **Avoid tobacco, alcohol, and drugs.**

Teresa & Jillian's Story

Teresa has been in early childhood for 15 years, and prior to working at LeapFrog, she was at a couple of schools with less than positive cultures. More often than not, to deal with the stress of her job, Teresa would drink several glasses of wine at the end of her workday. Over time, it had become a tough habit to break.

Teresa knew deep down inside that this habit was not good for her since it caused her to put on some weight and feel poorly about herself on the inside. She also had too many mornings that were tough to get out of bed because of the drinking.

Teresa was scrolling through Facebook one evening and saw an ad for a program called *"One Year No Beer"* with a 30-day challenge. She wondered to herself, *"Could I go booze-free for 30 days?"* She watched the videos of other women that had gone for a whole year and the Before and After photos of them were amazing. The After photos showed a huge shift – gone were the *"pudgy"* look in their faces, their eyes were brighter, their bodies were slimmer, and their faces showed huge smiles due to improved confidence and self-esteem.

Teresa decided to give it a try, just for 30 days. She joined the challenge. As of the writing of this book, she is on Day 66 with no alcohol. She feels great, has dropped a dress size, has much more clarity and patience in the classroom, more energy, and is a more optimistic, confident person. She's getting much better quality sleep and no more groggy mornings. She takes one day at a time and is challenging herself to see how far she can go.

For more information, visit OneYearNoBeer.com. The authors of this book do not endorse nor are affiliated with the One Year No Beer program.

Gem #14

Turn Off Your Darn Cell Phone

"The cell phone has become the adult's transitional object, replacing the toddler's teddy bear for comfort and a sense of belonging."

~ Margaret Heffernan

Nothing has done more damage to the self-image of young people today that the use of social media, and more importantly, its easy accessibility on a cell phone.

> *We want you to turn your cell phone off for two hours each day, preferably beginning two hours prior to bedtime.*

Today's kids don't verbally communicate, they text. They share every aspect of their life with total strangers and are judged by the number of likes they receive.

The truth is that the vast majority of people embellish posts on social media. No one ever posts the bad stuff, only the good stuff. Pictures are photoshopped, stories are fabricated, and everyone else's life seems to be so darn perfect except for yours. The truth is, their life is exactly the same as yours: they are lying.

We feel so sorry for kids growing up today with such low self-worth. Many of you reading this book were teenagers just a few short years ago. You still have feelings of low self-worth that I will help you to improve in the chapter on Mindset.

We want you to turn your cell phone off for two hours each day, preferably beginning two hours prior to bedtime. This will allow your brain to begin the shutdown procedure it needs to be able to properly rest overnight. The blue light from your cell phone interferes with your natural melatonin levels, which will disrupt your sleep and cause you to not become fully rested.

Substitute your cell phone time before bed with reading positive books to improve your mindset and your feeling of self-worth. Doing so will completely change your life for the better. If you don't believe us, just try it for 30 days. Call it *"Kris & Brian's 30-day Challenge,"* and let us know how you feel at the end of the challenge!

Remember this important gem on health and wellness: **Turn off your darn cell phone.**

Chapter 2 Notes:

_____

_____

_____

_____

_____

_____

_____

_____

_____

_____

_____

_____

_____

Chapter 3

Goals and Dreams

"Stay focused, go after your dreams and keep moving toward your goals."

~ LL Cool J

Dreams are a dime a dozen, everyone has them. Just ask someone buying a lottery ticket when the jackpot is super huge and you will hear a dream. We are sorry to tell you that dreams do not come true, that is until you attach a goal and a date to them.

To turn your dreams into action you must first set a goal and have a structured plan to achieve the goal, thus achieving the dream. Goals must have an action component to them, or they are just a dream.

You can be inspired by a dream, but goals can change the direction of your life for the positive. Here are 5 main differences between goals and dreams:

1. Dreams exist only in the mind; goals require an action of some kind.

2. Dreams do not have a timeline; goals have a deadline.

3. Dreams have no plan; goals have a plan to accomplish

them.

4. Dreams require little or no effort on your part; goals are hard work.

5. Dreams are free; you have to pay a hefty price for your goals.

So start with a dream, something as simple as "*I want to visit the Grand Canyon someday.*" Then take that dream and set a goal. Your goal needs a plan and a deadline. "*I will save $50 a week for two years and save up my vacation time to visit the Grand Canyon in the summer of 2021.*"

Notice the dream did not have a specific plan of achieving it. It was just a dream. The goal has a plan for success and a deadline for achieving it. Now spend some time writing down five dreams you have always wanted to accomplish in your life.

1. _____

2. _____

3. _____

4. _____

5. _____

Over the next few pages, we will help you to turn these dreams into reality by setting goals on how to obtain them. Please share these dreams with your boss. A good boss will always want to know the dreams of his or her employees.

Gem #15

Begin With the End in Mind

"Setting goals is the first step in turning the invisible into the visible."

~ Tony Robbins

When you set a goal, you should first start in your mind with a deadline on when you wish to achieve the goal, then start working backward. You do not have to do it this way, it is just something that has worked well in both of our lives. We like to picture ourselves achieving the goal so we have a mental picture of what success looks like, then we start putting the processes in place on how to make that picture a reality. We always begin with the end in mind.

If you fail to plan, you are planning to fail.

You should set some long-term goals for your life as well: retirement, homeownership, vacations, investments, family, etc. It is never too early to start setting goals for these items that may be 50 years away.

If you fail to plan, you are planning to fail. The majority of people in this world are not goal setters, and only about 3% of people actually write down their goals. Of the people that write down their goals, a vast majority of them actually achieve them. You miss 100% of the targets you fail to aim at!

Remember this important gem on goals and dreams: **Begin with the end in mind.**

Gem #16

Set Big, Hairy, Audacious Goals

"Set your goals high, and don't stop till you get there."

~ Bo Jackson

A goal should stretch you, and scare you a little. It is okay if it scares you a lot. For many of you reading this book, a high school diploma was once a goal for you. Some of you reading this book set a goal to have a college degree. Others may have had the goal to get married and raise a family.

Set your goals high, very high. Thomas Edison failed over 10,000 times to invent the light bulb. When interviewed, a reporter asked him how it felt to fail over 9,000 times and if he felt like a failure. His response? Quite the contrary. *"I have found 9,000 ways that do not work."* You will only fail if you quit trying. Thankfully, Thomas Edison did not quit because then maybe you would be reading this book by candlelight right now.

> *If there is no one laughing at your goals and dreams, they are not big enough!*

If there is no one laughing at your goals and dreams, they are not big enough! A goal must cause you to stretch harder than you ever have before, or obtaining it will not seem as sweet. A goal is like a rubber band; it works best if it is stretched.

So don't be afraid to set big, hairy, audacious goals and prepare to have the most amazing life you ever have imagined. No great accomplishment in human history has ever been successful without someone setting a goal that stretched them way out of their comfort zone. Enjoy the journey!

Remember this important gem on goals and dreams: **Set big, hairy, audacious goals.**

Teresa & Jillian's Story

Both Teresa and Jillian aren't so sure about setting big goals. Neither of them has ever been big on goal-setting. Sometimes it just seems easier to avoid the disappointment of dreams you can't reach – why set yourself up for failure?

Their director Donna talked to them about setting professional and personal goals for the coming year, since it was December and the new year was around the corner. After attending a goal-setting webinar, both ladies were encouraged and decided to give it a try, but they wanted to start with smaller bite-size goals, then work their way up.

Teresa had always wanted to travel to Italy, so she set that as a goal for 18 months in the future. Jillian had a goal to buy a new car and pay cash for it, rather than being on a payment plan. Both dreams seemed huge and even impossible when they first dared to imagine them. It was a little scary!

Gem #17

Set S.M.A.R.T Goals

"All who have accomplished great things have had a great aim, have fixed their gaze on a goal which was high, one which sometimes seemed impossible."

~ *Orison Swett Marden*

To know if a goal is a goal or just a dream, you can use the S.M.A.R.T criteria. S.M.A.R.T. stands for Specific, Measurable,

Achievable, Realistic, and Time-Specific. The first known use of the term occurs in the November 1981 issue of Management Review by George T. Doran.

When you are setting a goal, be sure to run the goal through the S.M.A.R.T. criteria.

1. **Specific:** Target a specific area of improvement.
2. **Measurable:** Quantity or at least suggest an indicator of progress.
3. **Achievable:** Able to be brought about or reached successfully.
4. **Realistic:** Can it reasonably be achieved within the available resources?
5. **Time-specific:** Must specify when it can be achieved.

> *When you are setting a goal, be sure to run the goal through the S.M.A.R.T. criteria.*

When you sit down to write your goals, take each one and give it the S.M.A.R.T. test. If it fails, you will need to alter the goal until it fits the criteria.

Remember this important gem on goals and dreams: **Set S.M.A.R.T. goals.**

Gem #18

Where Will You be Five Years From Now?

"Goals. There's no telling what you can do when you get inspired by them. There's no telling what you can do when you believe in them. And there's no telling what will happen when you act upon them."

~ Jim Rohn

Take a moment right now to look back at the last five years of your life. Are you where you expected to be at this point in your life? Did you have a goal of getting to where you are now that you set at some point in the past?

Five years will come and go before you know it. Where will you be five years from today?

The last five years more than likely flew by; they always do. The older you get, the faster they go, trust us. If you are not where you wanted to be at this point in your life, what is the reason? Did you have a goal and a plan for getting there? If not, now is the time to change.

Five years will come and go before you know it. Where will you be then? The time to set a goal to help you get where you wish to be in five years is now.

Use the criteria we gave you in the past few gems to help you set some goals and get to work. We want you to write them in this book because you have to write your goals down or you will never achieve them.

Today's Date: _____

Five years from today I will: _____

Is the goal S.M.A.R.T? If so, congratulations! Now set a detailed plan in motion and go make it happen. When you see us at a child care conference, please come up and tell us what your five-year goal is. We cannot wait to cheer for your success!

Remember this important gem on goals and dreams: **Where will you be five years from today?**

Gem #19

Write Down Your Goals and Post Them Everywhere!

"By recording your dreams and goals on paper, you set in motion the process of becoming the person you most want to be. Put your future in good hands—your own."

~ Mark Victor Hansen

If you were to walk into Kris or Brian's office, you would notice there are goals written on the walls. If you were to walk into our bathrooms, you would see goals taped to our bathroom mirrors. You need to write your goals out and post them everywhere.

> *You need to write your goals out and post them everywhere... There is power in writing down your goals.*

Why is it important to write down your goals and look at them often? First of all, your brain sees things consciously and subconsciously. When we look at a picture or a goal and actually think of it while we are looking at it, we are using our conscious. Our conscious mind is the most vulnerable to doubt and negative thoughts. We may look at a goal using conscious thought and deep down think it may be unobtainable.

On the other hand, our subconscious does not know the difference between the truth and a lie, and it thinks you can accomplish anything. By posting your goals everywhere, your subconscious mind will see them and will begin to work at finding a way to help you achieve them. There is power in writing down your goals.

When you write down a goal make sure you write it as you already have it accomplished. Some examples may be:

1. I weigh 125 pounds.
2. I have $10,000 in my savings account.
3. I am on the Dean's List with a 4.0 GPA.
4. I own a brand new white GMC Yukon.

The more specific you can be the better. Almost every goal that we both have set has come true when we did this. We recommend the book *Think and Grow Rich,* by Napoleon Hill. He wrote a lot about the success of this concept.

Take a few minutes and write down five goals. Be sure to write them as if they have already been accomplished:

1. _____

2. _____

3. _____

4. _____

5. _____

Congratulations! You are well on your way to achieving your goals in life. Be sure to post these goals everywhere, and go to work at making them come true. If you reach a goal you set, be sure to come to the Child Care Mindset Academy Group on Facebook and let us know about it! We are proud of you but, more than that, you should be so very proud of yourself!

Remember this important gem on goals and dreams: **Write down your goals and post them everywhere.**

Teresa & Jillian's Story

Teresa wrote down her goals for the coming year and made sure they were "**S.M.A.R.T.**" For her goal to visit Italy in 18 months, she needed to lay out a plan to save $6,000 for the trip. She and her husband agreed to sock away $200 a month by using coupons and cutting back on dinners at restaurants. They also were expecting a nice holiday bonus from her husband's company that they would use to start their *vacation savings account.* Teresa took a leap of faith and wrote down her goals, made copies, and pasted them in her closet, on her bathroom mirror, and in her car.

After six months, Teresa and her hubby, Tom, saved $2,000 towards their romantic Italian vacation. She was so excited and, since progress was being made every month toward the goal, it started to seem real. She knew she would hit the goal and her confidence around goal-setting improved.

Gem #20

Take Clarity Breaks

"Do something nice for yourself today. Find some quiet, sit in stillness, and breathe. Put your problems on pause. You deserve a break."

~ Akiroq Brost

In today's world, we never get a break. Our phones, tablets, laptops, watches, and smart home devices are constantly keeping us connected with the world, but this is not always a good thing.

A clarity break is a time each week where you can sit, walk, or jog all by yourself with no technology whatsoever. Leave all devices at home and go spend some time with the most important person in your life that can make all of your dreams and goals come true... You!

Use this time to think about your goals and dreams. Use this time to be thankful for the many blessings you have. You will learn in a later gem to have a thankfulness journal: be sure to take this on your clarity break and read some of your entries to help you remember what you are thankful for.

Block 30 minutes one day a week for a clarity break, it will change your life, we promise!

Taking a clarity break is good for stress relief. Many of you will tell us you do not have time; that is simply not true. We all have the same amount of time; it is how we utilize that time that is important. Block 30 minutes one day each week for a clarity break, it will change your life, we promise!

Remember this important gem on goals and dreams: **Take clarity breaks.**

Gem #21

Have a Dream Journal

"We all have dreams. But in order to make dreams come into reality, it takes an awful lot of determination, dedication, self-discipline, and effort."

~ Jesse Owens

At the beginning of this chapter, we asked you to write down five dreams, but we are confident that you can think of 95 more if you had a lot of quality time to think about it.

We would like you to buy a dream journal. This must be a hardcover book that will record your lifetime of dreams and accomplishments. We want to warn you that having a dream journal will completely change your life, and cause you to accomplish more in your life than you ever would without it.

> *"Whatever the mind of man can conceive and believe it can achieve"*
>
> *~Napoleon Hill*

When you get your journal, you will need to plan one to two hours of complete silence for your mind to be able to dream effectively. Start by spending 15 minutes just relaxing and clearing your mind. Use meditation techniques to get into a total state of relaxation. Make sure there is no way for you to be interrupted: phones turned off, and if you have children, make sure they are in bed for the evening.

After your relaxation time, turn to page one and start listing anything you wish to do before you die. Do not write details about the dream, that is what you do when you set goals to accomplish your dreams. Just jot down the first 100 things that come to mind.

Here are some topics that you may wish to have dreams about, but please do not let this limit you. Keep in mind, one of our favorite quotes from Napoleon Hill is, *"Whatever the mind of man can conceive and believe, it can achieve"*.

- Travel
- Financial
- Adventure
- Family
- Household
- Spiritual
- Educational
- Health
- Material things

When you get to 100, congratulations! You are well on your way to living a much more fulfilling life full of accomplishing your dreams. Only a small handful of the population writes down their goals and dreams; it is no wonder that only a small percentage of people actually obtain their dreams in life.

Pick the one dream you want to do the most, and then write a detailed plan to accomplish it. Set some goals for how you obtain it and get to work! Do the same with all of the goals. You can be working towards dozens of goals simultaneously! Just make sure that when you set your goals to accomplish your dreams, you use the methods we suggest in the previous gems on goal setting.

Remember this important gem on goals and dreams: **Have a dream journal.**

Chapter 3 Notes:

Chapter 4

Mindset

"Once your mindset changes, everything on the outside will change along with it."

~ *Steve Maraboli*

The next chapter takes up almost half of this book. There is an important reason for that, without the proper mindset you will never reach your full potential. Dreams, goals, and even your health all require a certain mindset to be fully realized. Change your mindset and you change your life!

Both Kris and Brian are the kind of coaches that do not pull our punches, so some of you reading this book may be upset by some of what you read. Some things may offend people or rub them the wrong way. The truth is, if we upset you temporarily and then you turn around and have an amazingly fulfilling life, full of obtaining your goals and dreams, well, we are okay with that.

We are not writing this book as your friend, we are writing this as your success coaches. You never want your coach telling you what you want to hear; you want your coach telling you how to make yourself better. That is what we are about to do here, make you better...mentally.

Your mind is amazing and can catapult you to greatness.

Your mind can also keep you locked in the chains of your own guilt, shame, and horrors. We highly recommend keeping a box of tissues handy, because we may hit a nerve or two. Please just trust us that on the other side of the book, an amazing life is waiting for you, providing you can change your mindset.

In each gem, we will be asking you to do things you are not going to want to do. If you trust us and act on 100% of the things we ask you to do in this chapter, your life will be completely changed in very short order and you will start living life up to your amazing potential.

Gem #22

The Past is in the Past

"Nothing that occurred in your past can have any influence over you except the influence that you allow it to have."

~ *Brian Tracy*

Today is a gift, that is why they call it the present. We were going to write about how each day we get to start with a clean slate, then we realized that many young people have no idea what a *slate* is.

Slate is what chalkboards used to be made of. Of course, many of you have never seen a chalkboard in school, you had dry erase markers. When we were kids, we had chalkboards. At the end of the day, you could erase everything on the board. Imagine how confusing it would be if we never erased the board and started fresh each day, we would be confused because we were living in the past.

Each day when you wake up, you can choose to live in the past or live in the present. Many of you reading this are living in the past. It is our hope that when you get done reading this book, you will start living in the present, and enjoy the gift.

Almost everyone reading this book has had something traumatic happen in your lifetime. Some of you have a disability that has caused you to think less of yourself; many of you have been sexually assaulted; some have been abused or neglected by a family member; some of you are victims of domestic violence either currently or in the past. Some of you even choose the child care field because you were abused as children and, in some way, by working with children you feel you are protecting them.

> *Each day when you wake up, you can choose to live in the past or live in the present.*

Some of you are self-medicating with alcohol, drugs, or sex in an effort to drown out feelings of low self-worth. Others have tried suicide or are contemplating suicide in an effort to stop the pain. If we have described you, we are so sorry this has happened to you.

We would like you to make a conscious choice to live differently and join us in making this choice. We want to give you a gift, and we want you to open it each and every morning when you wake up. The gift is your present. Each day you can open it and start over, writing on your own slate. Whatever happens to you today, don't worry about it: tomorrow you get a clean slate.

Living for today will change your life. It gives you all of the control and robs your past of all of the power it has over you. No longer will you be chained to the shame and guilt of your yesterdays; you are free to live your present as the gift it was intended to be.

Remember this important gem for having an amazing mindset: **The past is in the past.**

Teresa & Jillian's Story

When Teresa read this gem, she felt like the authors were talking directly to her. You see, Teresa experienced a fairly traumatic childhood. At work, no one except Donna knew about her troubled past. Teresa's father was an abusive alcoholic, and Teresa witnessed the abuse of her mother at her father's hand. Teresa herself was also a target of the abuse, although more verbal than physical. This made Teresa's drinking issues even more damaging to her self-worth because she could see herself repeating her father's behavior.

Fortunately, Teresa's mother moved across the country and took the kids with her when Teresa was in middle school. Life drastically improved, so Teresa had a model for how trauma in life can be turned around. However, it certainly took its toll. Teresa feels she can get overly stressed in high-energy situations and is sometimes socially awkward or even anxious.

Reading about her life in this chapter as a *"Gift"* and opening her *"Present"* every day helped remind Teresa to work on letting go of the past and moving forward into her great future. She was able to work on being grateful for each day and break free of her traumatic past just a little more every day. She decided to earmark and re-read this chapter at stressful times or when she felt the anxiety creeping in.

Gem #23

Smile in the Mirror

"Smile in the mirror. Do that every morning and you'll start to see a big difference in your life."

~ Yoko Ono

We would like you to find a mirror, walk up to it, and spend two minutes smiling at yourself in the mirror. You are not going to want to do this. Please put this book down and find a mirror: this is very important.

- What did you see?
- Did it feel strange to smile at yourself?
- Did it make you feel a little better about yourself?

Those of you who did not do this (We know many of you did not try this), please go do it now. The rest of us will wait for you. No cheating, we are watching you!

> *Your brain will start equating smiling at yourself as a sign that you are happy with yourself.*

What we would like you to do now is get a paper and pen and write the word SMILE! and tape it to your bathroom mirror.

We would like you to smile at yourself each morning before you go to work for at least one minute and also one minute before you go to bed. We can promise you that you will feel weird doing it, but if you trust me your life will change.

Your brain will start equating smiling at yourself as a sign that you are happy with yourself. Many of you reading this chapter do not like what you see in the mirror. We are going to change that right now.

Remember this important gem for having an amazing mindset: **Smile in the mirror at least twice a day.**

Gem #24

FLY (First Love Yourself)

"Love yourself first and everything else falls into line. You really have to love yourself to get anything done in this world."

~ Lucille Ball

Now that we are beginning to put the past in the past, and we can look in the mirror and smile at ourselves it is time to begin to fall in love again, with yourself.

Brian's wife, Carol, wanted a butterfly tattoo. She designed it and had the tattoo artist write the word *"FLY"* under it, as a daily reminder to first love yourself.

It is impossible to love others if you cannot love yourself.

If you are a Christian and have a problem loving yourself first, then reword it so that only after God, you love yourself first.

It is impossible to love others if you cannot love yourself.

We have met so many people in our lives that literally hate themselves. Most are living in the past, and we took care of that in Gem #22.

Do us a favor and say out loud to yourself right now, *"I love myself."*

Now I know only about 1/3 of you actually did it, we will all wait while the rest of you do this exercise; it is very important. Say *"I LOVE MYSELF"* out loud.

How do you feel right now? Say it again this time louder! Does it make you feel better? We bet it did.

Remember this important gem for having an amazing mindset: **First love yourself.**

Gem #25

Master Positive Self-Talk

"Positive self-talk is to emotional pain as pain pill is to physical pain."

~ *Edmond Mbiaka*

You spend a large part of your day talking to yourself without even realizing you are doing it. Unfortunately, most people's self-talk is dangerously self-destructive.

> *You spend a large part of your day talking to yourself without even realizing you are doing it.*

Your brain does not know the difference between the truth and a lie, so when you speak with negative self-talk your brain believes it as the truth. *"You dummy." "You idiot." "I am so dumb." "I am so ugly."* Have you ever said such words to yourself? Most people have at some point; others say these things (and much worse) on a daily basis.

Positive self-talk is a great way to help you love yourself and will also help you keep the past in the past. Whenever you notice yourself saying anything negative internally, immediately correct it by drowning it out with positive self-talk.

We are going to try an experiment. We want you to repeat some words out loud. Say these words loudly: *"I am awesome!"* *"I am amazing!"* *"I feel great!"* *"I am a winner!"* *"Everyone loves me!"* *"I am lean, mean and super sexy!"* *"I love myself!"*

Now that everyone at the coffee shop you are reading this book in is staring at you, realize one thing: who cares! You are amazing. Why not tell the world? There is no one in the world exactly like you.

Remember this important gem for having an amazing mindset: **Master positive self-talk.**

Teresa & Jillian's Story

After they read this gem, Jillian and Teresa started listening more closely to each others' use of language about themselves in the classroom. One day Jillian showed up late as she had forgotten to set her alarm clock and overslept. She said *"I'm such an idiot! Duh!"* as she bounced into the classroom, about 30 minutes late. Teresa said nothing and just smiled.

Later, during nap time, Teresa whispered to Jillian, *"Hey, about this morning. You called yourself an idiot and I just want you to know you're clearly NOT an idiot. You're a great teacher and very smart. We all have times when we forget stuff. So watch that negative self-talk!"* They laughed about the idea of saying in front of their men, *"I'm lean, mean, and super sexy!"* Jillian actually dared Teresa to go do that some evening while snuggling on the couch with her husband, Tom.

Both ladies became more aware of their internal and external self-talk, and occasionally called each other out with the goal of being more positive in their thoughts, words, habits, and behaviors.

Gem #26

You Are Special

"Always remember that you are absolutely unique. Just like everyone else."

~ Margaret Mead

At the Kris Murray Child Care Success Summit in 2018, Les Brown was the celebrity keynote speaker and the theme of his talk was *"You are Special."*

There has never, nor will there ever in the history of this universe, be another you.

Les Brown has an amazing ability to make an audience feel special. We are by no means trying to steal any of his thunder here by talking about this topic, quite the contrary. We are honoring him by sharing the framework for his existence; his foster mom let him know from an early age how special he was.

You are special. There has never, nor will there ever in the history of this universe, be another you. You are one in a hundred million billion trillion, which makes you pretty darn special in our book.

Think of the odds of your being born. It is astronomical to think of the thousands of ancestors that had to have babies that grew up to have babies to eventually get to your parents and out of all of the billions of sperm and thousands of eggs, the perfect two just happen to meet to create you. Did we happen to mention the billions of sperm and millions of eggs of all of your ancestors had to be timed perfectly as well? One headache amongst any of your ancestors on conception night in the last ten thousand years and you would never have been born. How is that for being special? The odds of your existence are about as much of a long shot as someone asked to pick out a particular grain of sand somewhere in the world and pick it correctly.

Once you realize how amazingly special you are, you will stop beating yourself up over your past and stop the negative. You will learn to love yourself first knowing that you are unique and amazing.

Remember this important gem for having an amazing mindset: **You are special.**

Gem #27

The Greatest Story Ever Told

"Everyone has a story to tell, a lesson to teach, and wisdom to share... Life is a beautiful masterpiece bound together by your experiences. Open up and share your story; become an inspiration to others. You can make a difference because you matter. You were created with a purpose. Live your life with intention, go out there and make a difference by being the difference."

~ Melanie Moushigian Koulouris

Would you want to read a book with the title, *"The Greatest Story Ever Told?"* Who wouldn't? It is the greatest story EVER told! Surely, it would be an international bestseller!

In 1976, Dr. John Maxwell received a book in the mail with the title *"The Greatest Story Ever Told."* Imagine his shock when he opened it to find all the pages blank-except for a note from the giver that said, *"John, your life is before you. Fill these pages with kind acts, good thoughts, and matters of your heart. Go write the Greatest Story Ever Told!"*

Dr. Maxwell did just that with his life: he has written more than 80 best-selling books that have changed the lives of millions of people.

We are asking you to do what Dr. Maxwell has done, go out and write the story of your life. Each day, you are blessed with a chance to start over and today is the first day of the rest of your life. It is time to write a story of significance and write your story with the ending you want, and we can promise you, it will be a happy ending.

> *Each day, you are blessed with a chance to start over and today is the first day of the rest of your life.*

Please pick up a notebook at an office supply store and write on the cover *The Greatest Story Ever Told* and begin writing the story of your life. What will your story be? You are the author: make it count.

Remember this important gem for having an amazing mindset: **Go write the greatest story ever told.**

Gem #28

Read *The Slight Edge* by Jeff Olson

"The truth is, what you do matters. What you do today matters. What you do every day matters. Successful people just do the things that seem to make no difference in the act of doing them and they do them over and over and over until the compound effect kicks in."

~ Jeff Olson

We have both read the book *The Slight Edge* by Jeff Olson. This book has fundamentally changed the way we both treat each day, how we tackle problems, and how we view the world. Moreover, the early childhood owners and leaders we've coached have cited *The Slight Edge* as THE book that's been the most impactful in their personal growth journey, more so than any other book.

Jeff Olson is a multi-millionaire businessman who has written a book that allows you to gain a very interesting perspective on mindset, goal setting, and consistency.

> *We guarantee that if you read The Slight Edge and apply what you learn, it will change your life, just like it did ours.*

We suggest that you take a moment right now and visit your favorite internet bookseller and order this book right away. It will be at your door in a few days, just about the time you are finishing this book. We guarantee that if you read *The Slight Edge* and apply what you learn, it will change your life, just like it did ours.

Remember this important gem for having an amazing mindset: **Read *The Slight Edge* by Jeff Olson.**

Teresa & Jillian's Story

Teresa and Jillian were having a great time reading inspiring books together as a mini-book club with all the other teachers in their company. They decided to give *The Slight Edge* by Jeff Olson a try. Director Donna ordered a copy for every teacher in the school, and off they went to dig into the book. Jillian had low expectations...how could a single book be THAT good?

They started out reading just 10 pages a day, to keep it simple, gain a consistent rhythm, and be on the same pace (see Gem #30). After a week of reading 10 pages, they were both 70 pages into the book and AMAZED at how they felt. They realized the importance of persistence and consistency.

They realized that most people don't make huge shifts in their life or reach important goals because most people only try for a handful of days or months, then they GIVE UP. They stop doing the daily habit that is sure to bring results, out of fear, boredom, hard work, or laziness. Not wanting to stick to it. *"No one else is working this hard, why should I?"*

Jillian was most impacted by the practice of putting pennies away every day for investing and reaching her financial goals. She made changes to her direct deposit accounts so that for every paycheck, $60 would automatically go into her new savings account. After a year, she would have $1,560 saved. She also started putting all her spare change into a milk jug in her home, and socked away an additional $50 a month in spare change, rolled up into coin holders. All in, that's $2,160 a year! She was planning to open a Roth IRA with the money, and start investing. She was excited to start listening to the Dave Ramsey financial radio show to learn more about saving.

Fast forward 10 years after you read this, Jillian's and Teresa's lives will be hugely impacted by *The Slight Edge*. How will your life be different, better, and more successful?

Gem #29

Join the Child Care Mindset Academy Facebook Group

"Most of the important things in the world have been accomplished by people who have kept on trying when there seemed no hope at all."

~ Dale Carnegie

Working in a child care setting can be stressful; we see it first hand each and every day. We also understand that many of you work in a negative setting and it is hard to have a positive mindset in such a negative environment.

We have created an amazing resource for you to get a little bit of positive feedback each and every day. Go to Facebook and type in Child Care Mindset Academy and request to join our group.

We understand that many of you work in a negative setting and it is hard to have a positive mindset...

What will you expect to see in this group? All positive, all of the time! If you are down, come to this page and get lifted up! We both run this group and this is where you can send us a direct message if we can help you in any way.

Remember this important gem for having an amazing mindset: **Join the Child Care Mindset Academy Facebook Group.**

Gem #30

Read Every Day in a PMA Book

"You can't buy happiness, but you can buy books and that's kind of the same thing."

~ Anonymous

PMA stands for Positive Mental Attitude. PMA was first introduced by Napoleon Hill in the 1937 book *Think and Grow Rich*. We highly recommend this book and have included it on our Recommended Reading List at the end of the book.

Positive mental attitude is the philosophy that having an optimistic outlook in every situation attracts a positive outcome.

Your brain is an incredible computer that relies on programming, very similar to a desktop computer. If a programmer programmed a computer to give you the wrong answers to every question you typed into it, the computer wouldn't be at fault, the computer programmer would be.

You are your brain's programmer, and frankly, if you're like the average person, you are not doing a great job at programming your brain. When was the last time you fed positive thoughts into your brain? Ever heard of the phrase *"Garbage in, garbage out?"*

> *The average person today will see more useless images in a day than someone 100 years ago saw in their entire lifetime.*

The average person today will see more useless images in a day than someone 100 years ago saw in their entire lifetime. We are programming our brains with useless garbage day in and day out.

There is nothing wrong with sitting down and watching a television show and we are not advocating eliminating this from your life. However, you should make it a priority to spend 15 - 30 minutes reading from a positive mental attitude book each day. By doing this you will totally change your mindset and learn how to tackle problems that you will face in life.

Make it a habit to read at least 10 pages a day in a PMA book. If you do not like to read, get the audiobook and listen to it while you drive to and from work. Creating this habit will change your life, we can promise you.

Remember this important gem for having an amazing mindset: **Read every day in a PMA book.**

Gem #31

Increase Your Self-Esteem

"Why should we worry about what others think of us, do we have more confidence in their opinions than we do our own?"

~ Brigham Young

Your self-esteem is your true opinion of yourself. Do you value yourself? Do you love yourself? Do you think you are an amazing teacher? Are you a happy person? Do you think your co-workers value your contribution to the team? Do you let other people's opinions get you down?

When we let other people's opinions of us get us down, we are giving them all of the power. Why should we trust their opinion more than our own? It is time to take back control of your own self-worth. It is time to learn how amazingly special you really are. In order to know what causes us to think less of ourselves, we have to understand what is triggering it.

> *When we let other people's opinions of us get us down, we are giving them all of the power.*

Some of the things that lower your self-esteem:

- Allowing someone to put you down or belittle you.
- Abuse or neglect somewhere in your past.
- Letting people take advantage of you.
- Working in a job that does not make you happy.

- Giving up on the dreams you have had in your life.
- Negative self-talk.
- Thinking everyone else on social media lives near-perfect lives.

Using the tools in this book will increase your self-esteem and help you learn to value yourself and your contribution to your child care setting.

Remember this important gem for having an amazing mindset: **Increase your self-esteem.**

Gem #32

Visioning is Very Important

"If you don't have a vision you're going to be stuck in what you know. And the only thing you know is what you've already seen."

~ Iyanla Vanzant

Your brain does not know the difference between the truth and a lie. Your brain is a computer, and as we discussed in this chapter on Mindset the programming of your brain is very important.

When you write down your goals, you need to picture yourself already in possession of whatever goal you have set for yourself. You need to tell your brain to picture it as though it's been accomplished.

Let's say you have a goal to weigh 125 pounds. You need to close your eyes and see yourself on a scale, with the number showing at 125. You need to say out loud, *"I weigh 125 pounds."* Each time you read your goals, you need to read them as if you are already in possession of the goal. This is called visioning, and it works!

Believe it, picture it, and then your brain will go to work making it come true. It does not know you have not attained it yet; your subconscious will work hard to manifest what you have envisioned.

Your friends and family will think you are a bit loony when they walk into a room and there you are with your eyes closed stating goals as if they've been accomplished already.

Your brain does not know the difference between the truth and a lie.

Do it right now, read each goal that you set in Chapter 3 and read them as if you've already completed those goals. This will greatly increase the likelihood of achieving them. Do this each and every day until your goals become your reality. This has worked for us in our lives over and over.

"Whatever the mind of man can conceive and believe, it can achieve"

~ Napoleon Hill.

Remember this important gem for having an amazing mindset: **Visioning is very important.**

Teresa & Jillian's Story

Teresa was familiar with the idea of visioning and *"manifesting your dreams."* She had a couple of girlfriends who got together about a year ago and they all spent an evening making vision boards as a fun group activity. Teresa went home and pulled out the vision board from her closet and dusted it off.

On her board were pictures of things she'd always dreamed

of, and images cut from travel magazines. A luxury car, a home with a pool and spa, and a trip to Italy. As she saw the images of Rome and Tuscany, she got a huge grin on her face. Because she and her hubby, Tom, had started saving (remember they put $600 a month away for their dream trip to Italy?), they were already HALFWAY to their goal! Her vision was becoming a reality before her eyes!

That night, Teresa had a vivid dream about Italy and woke up with excitement – she couldn't wait to tell Jillian about her dream! The teachers later had an in-depth conversation about using visioning and vision boards to help manifest their dreams. They decided to talk to Donna about doing a vision board crafting activity with all their fellow teachers, during their next staff meeting.

Gem #33

Use Subliminal Messaging

"Our subliminal mental processes operate outside awareness because they arise in these portions of our mind that are inaccessible to our conscious self; their inaccessibility is due to the architecture of the brain rather than because they have been subject to Freudian motivational forces like repression."

~ Leonard Mlodinow

I am awesome! I am special! I am beautiful! I am smart! I am an amazing teacher! Everyone loves me! I am happy! I love me! My kids love me! My family loves me! I love my body!

When you read that, how did it make you feel? You read it as though you were talking to yourself. Did doing so make you feel better? happier? Repeating positive words to yourself will release dopamine and make you feel better.

We would recommend downloading a subliminal message app on your phone and have positive sayings rotated so that your brain will *"see them"* and you won't even know you are reading them.

We would also recommend putting positive notes around your home: on your bathroom mirror, on your car dashboard, on your computer screen, and on your refrigerator. The more notes you put up, the more your brain will see without you even being aware of them.

> *Repeating positive words to yourself will release dopamine and make you feel better.*

Remember this important gem for having an amazing mindset: **Use subliminal messaging.**

Gem #34

Stop Hanging Around Negative People

"You cannot expect to live a positive life if you hang with negative people."

~ Joel Osteen

Your income, attitude, and mindset manifest in direct proportion to the five people you hang around with the most. Look at the five friends you spend the most time with and see if this is true.

When you put a crab into a bowl he will just crawl out. How do you get a crab to stay in a pot? You put another crab in with him.

Once the crab starts to crawl out, the other one will drag

him back in as he tries to get out. If each of them were to work together, they both could get out, but they will kill each other trying to make sure the other one does not succeed.

Your income, attitude, and mindset are in direct proportion to the five people you hang around with the most.

Many of your friends are crabs. They are negative people and they are happiest when they are complaining about something. If you start displaying a positive mindset, they will be just like the crab trying to bring you down to their level. They do not want you to get out of the negativity bowl.

Social media has a great feature to eliminate negativity from your life; it is called UNFRIEND. Life is too short to hang around people that do not support you.

Remember this important gem for having an amazing mindset: **Stop hanging around negative people.**

Teresa & Jillian's Story

Jillian and Teresa were determined to stay positive, kind, and supportive with each other so they could both reach their goals in and out of the classroom. However, it sometimes proved difficult when hanging out with other staff members. Most of the team were happy, positive people, but two of their co-workers, in particular, seemed to be the "*crabs*" of the school – determined to drag the others down to the bottom of the pot. The more people they could bring over to "*the dark side*," the better.

That week, a particularly difficult staff meeting took place in which these two teachers caused dissent and friction with their constant complaining and negativity. The next day, Jillian and Teresa dreaded coming to work. Much to their surprise, when they showed up to work, they were told that the "*degrading duo*" had been fired. Hooray! Both ladies gave huge hugs to Donna for having the courage to finally let these Negative Nellies go. Everyone pitched in with extra hours for the next 10 days until replacements could be on-boarded and trained. The school culture improved immediately and the team is now renewed with a sense of purpose, passion, and positivity.

Gem #35

Be Confident

"No one can make you feel inferior without your consent."

~ Eleanor Roosevelt

It does not matter if you are a teacher's aide, a teacher, the cook, a janitor, the assistant director, the director, the executive director or the owner, you need to be confident in everything that you do.

You were hired to do a very important job. No matter if this is the job you have dreamed of doing your whole life or it is a stepping stone to something different, you need to be confident in your ability to do the best job each and every day.

> *Confidence is a very important key to success.*

Confidence is a very important key to success. You should work as though you are the most important member of your child care team because you are. You were hired because you possessed a particular talent that not many people on this planet have, the ability to pass on knowledge to another person.

So the next time you go to work, be confident that what you

are doing is making a huge difference in the lives of so many, including the owner of your center. Hold your head up high, because you are a hero to us and so many other people.

Remember this important gem for having an amazing mindset: **Be confident.**

Gem #36
Don't Worry - Be Happy!

"If you want happiness for an hour - take a nap.

If you want happiness for a day - go fishing.

If you want happiness for a year - inherit a fortune.

If you want happiness for a lifetime - help someone else."

~ *Chinese Proverb*

If you want happiness for a lifetime, help someone else. Isn't that what you do each and every day? Happiness is a state of mind, but you control the state you are in.

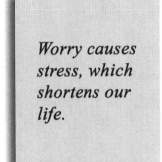

Worry causes stress, which shortens our life.

Why do you worry? Because you have a negative mindset and you are expecting the worst. How many times have you worried that something bad would happen and everything was fine? Worry causes stress, which shortens our life. Not worrying and expecting a positive outcome will not change what would have happened; it will cause you to live a happier, longer life.

So the next time something in your life causes you to want

to worry, turn that frown upside down and choose to be happy and have a positive attitude, expecting a positive outcome. Worry causes us to lose sleep, overeat, and be less productive at work and at home. We firmly believe that it's possible to manifest a positive outcome with positive expectations.

Remember this important gem for having an amazing mindset: **Don't worry – be happy!**

Gem #37

Life is Not Fair

"The world is not fair, and often fools, cowards, liars and the selfish hide in high places."

~ Bryant H. McGill

If life were fair, it would be boring! If life were fair we would all be driving the same car, making the same wage, having the same amount of children, having the same profession.

The truth is you never want life to be fair, you want to go out and create the life you want instead of being jealous of someone else for having it.

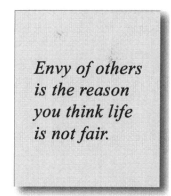

Envy of others is the reason you think life is not fair.

Envy of others is the reason you think life is not fair. You look at another person and are jealous of what they have or have done. It is time to stop that stinking thinking and go find a way to get what YOU want in life.

If you were to look back at the history of every person who has accomplished amazing things in life, you will find someone who has had to go through exactly what you have had to and persevered anyway.

Go back to the chapter on goals and dreams and set yourself on a course to get what you want in life. Stop looking at other people's situations and start focusing on your own. You are the master of your own fate. You are not a victim; you are a winner. Stop blaming other people for your situation, own your own life and go out there and make a difference. We believe in you.

Remember this important gem for having an amazing mindset: **Life is not fair.**

Gem #38

Keep a Gratitude Journal

"Thankfulness creates gratitude which generates contentment that causes peace."

~ *Todd Stocker*

Take a moment right now and write out ten things you are grateful for:

1. _____

2. _____

3. _____

4. _____

5. _____

6. _____

7. _____

8. _____

9. _____

10. _____

Was it hard to write things you are thankful for? Probably not. We want you to put this book down, go to an online ordering site, and order a journal.

Each day when you get up, we would like you to write one thing you are thankful for in this journal.

There are going to be tough times ahead, it happens to everyone. No one gets through this life without encountering problems. Let us show you how to get through those rough patches.

> *There are going to be tough times ahead, it happens to everyone.*

When life hands you a challenge, when you start having negative thoughts, when you start feeling sorry for yourself, when things seem at their worst, it is time to pull out your gratitude journal and start reading.

Your brain cannot have a negative and positive thought simultaneously. By filling your mind with positive thoughts, you will be diluting your brain and changing your mindset. If you were thinking about things you are thankful for, it would be impossible for you to feel sorry for yourself at the same time.

Remember this important gem for having an amazing mindset: **Have a gratitude journal.**

Gem #39

Listen to Positive Podcasts

"You can't make positive choices for the rest of your life without an environment that makes those choices easy, natural, and enjoyable."

~ Deepak Chopra

One way to make positive choices in your life is to listen to positive podcasts and positive audiobooks. If you spend a lot of time commuting, your car can become a rolling university; giving you a degree in positivity.

> *One podcast we would highly recommend listening to is Child Care Rockstar Radio, hosted by Kris Murray.*

There are many positive podcasts out there for you to listen to. Go to the Apple Store or the Google Play Store and subscribe to your favorite.

One podcast we would highly recommend listening to is Child Care Rockstar Radio, hosted by Kris Murray. Every other week she interviews childcare owners, directors, and leaders of the child care industry.

Find time to listen to positive podcasts and positive audiobooks: while you are on a treadmill, working out, making dinner, or driving, use that time wisely and put something positive in your brain. You won't have to take any of your precious time, and you will be a much happier person for it.

Remember this important gem for having an amazing mindset: **Listen to positive podcasts.**

Gem #40

Beware of the Power of the Tongue

"You are snared by the words of your mouth."

~ Proverbs 6:2 NKJV

There are life and death in the power of the tongue. Words matter. Think back to a time in your life when someone said something to you that hurt you in some way. Sometimes words can cause more hurt to you than a physical injury.

The same thing is true for words we speak to other people. We must guard our words carefully and be sure to think before we talk. We must never gossip about someone else or use words to cause hurt to him or her. We need to choose to use words to uplift others at every opportunity.

We must guard our words carefully and be sure to think before we talk.

We must also apply this same principle to the words we say to ourselves. Our self-talk must be guarded as to always be uplifting and never hurtful. We would highly recommend the book *What You Say When You Talk to Yourself*, by Shad Helmstetter, Ph.D. as a great guide on how to talk to yourself.

Remember this important gem for having an amazing mindset: **Beware of the power of the tongue.**

Gem #41

Practice Random Acts of Kindness

"Beginning today, treat everyone you meet as if they were going to be dead by midnight. Extend to them all the care, kindness and understanding you can muster, and do it with no thought of any reward. Your life will never be the same again."

~ Og Mandino

Have you ever randomly done something nice for someone without ever expecting to be acknowledged for the act? That is a true random act of kindness.

Please choose to be a giver, practice random acts of kindness and make someone else feel special.

Buy the coffee for the car behind you at a drive-thru coffee shop. Pay for the toll for the car behind you the next time you are on a highway. Send notes to the parents of your students telling them how amazing they are. Make someone else's day with little effort on your part.

You see, in this world there are givers and there are takers. Please choose to be a giver, practice random acts of kindness and make someone else feel special. We can promise you that in your heart, you will be the biggest beneficiary of your kind gesture.

You don't have to spend money to practice random acts of kindness. You can rake a neighbor's yard, send a handwritten card to a friend, hold the door for a stranger, or volunteer at a homeless shelter. There are millions of ways you can help someone else. We promise you, making someone else feel special is an amazing feeling.

Remember this important gem for having an amazing mindset: **Practice random acts of kindness.**

Teresa & Jillian's Story

One of the things that Jillian loves the most about working at LeapFrog is the positive culture of kindness. It's led from the top by Donna, who as the director, spends a lot of time doing random acts of kindness for her team. She gives gift cards, celebrates small and large victories, brings treats and food for the teacher break room, does Pizza Fridays a couple of times a month, leaves notes and cards for staff, and more.

Thinking about this gem and the school culture that she loved inspired Jillian to do more random acts of kindness. One day, she started making a little list of *"kindness ideas"* on her phone and used it to actively do little surprises for friends, loved ones, and strangers. She sent flowers to her mom for no reason. She brought her boyfriend his favorite sandwich for lunch one day at work. She even went out of her comfort zone and bought coffee for the person behind her in line at Starbucks. These little joy-spreading activities made Jillian feel like a million bucks as she realized the power of giving to others.

Gem #42

I am AWESOME!

"Optimism is the onne quaity more associated with success and happiness than any other."

~ *Brian Tracy*

Say these words to yourself, *"I am awesome!"* Does it sound a little weird? Does it make you feel a little awesomer? Now, we know that is not a real word, we just made it up but since this is our book, we get to do that. LOL is not a real word and most people use it every day, so why can't we make up a word?

We hope you have been proactive in improving your mindset by actually writing in this book as you read it. You will get the most out of it by doing so. We are going to ask you to do something now that you are not going to want to do. Please trust me that it is important for your overall mindset.

> *Your brain cannot have a negative and a positive thought simultaneously...*

We want you to pull out your cell phone and turn it on. We know you have had it turned off while reading this book since you would never want to be interrupted.

We want you to record yourself reading some phrases that we ask you to, all while looking into the camera.

Are you ready? Some of you are hesitating; please trust us on this. Get your cell out and record yourself; it will be worth it.

Press record and say the following:

- I AM AWESOME!
- I FEEL GREAT!
- I AM A WINNER!
- EVERYONE LOVES ME!
- I AM SO GOOD LOOKING!
- EVERYONE LOVES BEING AROUND ME!
- I AM A WONDERFUL PERSON!
- I LOVE ME!
- I AM AWESOME!

You can now stop recording. How do you feel? We bet you feel much better than you did before! Remember your brain does not know the difference between the truth and a lie and you just told your brain how you feel. It will then secrete the right hormones to make sure you have those positive feelings.

The next time you are down; the next time you feel depressed; the next time you are sad; pull your phone out and watch yourself telling you how amazing you are. You will immediately begin to feel better. Your brain cannot have a negative and a positive thought simultaneously, so you can make your brain think positive thoughts and bury the negative ones. When you do this life starts getting much better.

Remember this important gem for having an amazing mindset: **I am AWESOME!**

Gem #43

Eliminating Fear is Important!

"I learned that courage was not the absence of fear, but the triumph over it. The brave man is not he who does not feel afraid, but he who conquers that fear."

~ Nelson Mandela

There is an amazing acronym that describes what fear really is:

F – False
E – Evidence
A – Appearing
R – Real

Fear knocked on the door, faith answered and there was no one there! Having faith will cure fear. Faith and fear cannot exist in the same thought.

We all have fears; some of us have more than others. Learning to overcome these fears is paramount to having an amazing mindset and obtaining the dreams and goals you have in life.

> *We all have fears; some of us have more than others.*

Some common fears include:

- **Fear of what others will think**

    This is where you worry about what other people will think if you post your goals around your house, start reading positive books, and unfriend a few Negative Nellies on social media.

- **Fear of failure**

    This is where you are afraid to fail. You will refuse to set a goal for fear of being let down if you do not achieve it. You are only a failure if you do not get up after you have been knocked down.

- **Fear of success**

    Believe it or not, some people are afraid of actually succeeding. The reason is that your self-image is so low you expect to fail at everything you do. As you implement the gems in this book, your self-image will improve significantly and success will be more within your grasp.

- **Fear of change**

    Change is hard. It takes 21 days of repetitive actions to create a habit. Most people tend to want to stay within their comfort zone with their actions. Remember this one important quote from Dr. John Maxwell: *"Life begins at the end of your comfort zone."*

Remember this important gem for having an amazing mindset: **Eliminating fear is important!**

Gem #44

Don't Sweat the Small Stuff

"One of the mistakes many of us make is that we feel sorry for ourselves, or for others, thinking that life should be fair, or that someday it will be. It's not and it won't. When we make this mistake we tend to spend a lot of time wallowing and/or complaining about what's wrong with life. "It's not fair," we complain, not realizing that, perhaps, it was never intended to be."

~ Richard Carlson, Don't Sweat the Small Stuff ... and it's all small stuff: Simple Ways to Keep the Little Things from Taking Over Your Life

How many times have you worried about something that turned out to be nothing? How many times have we worried about little things that are really insignificant in the overall scheme of life?

> *How many times have you worried about something that turned out to be nothing?*

Worry causes stress which will shorten your life. Take control of your life by refusing to allow yourself to be controlled by worry and fear.

How many times have you fought with your significant other over things that later seemed completely foolish to be quarreling over?

The secret to this gem is treating everything in your life as small stuff, and not sweating it. Never let things you cannot control have power over your thoughts and actions. It is time to take your life back. Worry and fear only have power over you if you let them.

Remember this important gem for having an amazing mindset: **Don't sweat the small stuff.**

Teresa & Jillian's Story

Teresa's mom Sylvia is a great lady. After she was able to escape her abusive marriage to Teresa's father, she created a safe and loving home for Teresa and her siblings. However, all the trauma that Sylvia suffered caused her to be anxious and spend a lot of time worrying. She worried about the weather. She worried about the kids and grandkids' safety from predators. She worried about the economy. She worried about the arguments coming from the next-door neighbor's house. Actually, there wasn't much that Sylvia did not worry about!

Teresa realized that the majority of things her mom worried about were imaginary fears that never came to pass. She brought this to Sylvia's attention and together they added up how many hours in a typical week were WASTED due to worry about things beyond Sylvia's control or things that simply never happened. It added up to 20-25 hours a week! What an incredible waste of time!

By shining a light on this issue, Teresa helped her mom gain powerful insight about sweating the small stuff. Now Sylvia tries to worry less and focus on the great things she has in her life. She keeps a gratitude journal, and whenever she starts worrying or being fearful, she reads the journal.

Gem #45

Never Go to Bed Angry

"For every minute you remain angry, you give up sixty seconds of peace of mind."

~ *Ralph Waldo Emerson*

The Bible speaks about the importance of not letting the sun go down on your anger, and regardless of whether you believe in God, we think this is really good advice. Make a point to have a deal with your partner that you will never go to bed angry at each other. Work hard to come up with compromises before you go to bed, and we can promise you that when you wake up things will be a whole lot better than going to bed angry.

This holds true for being angry with a co-worker or a friend. Always try to resolve issues the same day, so you don't carry anger around with you. Going to bed angry will disrupt your sleep cycle making you more tired the next day, and less effective in your job in early childhood education. You need to always be at the top of your game.

> *Make a point to have a deal with your partner that you will never go to bed angry at each other.*

If you are married, or in a serious long term relationship we would highly recommend the book *His Needs, Her Needs* by Willard F. Harley, Jr. We highly recommend both partners getting their own copies of the book and taking notes in it.

Remember this important gem for having an amazing mindset: **Never go to bed angry.**

Gem #46

Have a Positive Classroom

"It's the teacher that makes the difference, not the classroom."

~ Michael Morpurgo

If you are a teacher, you are spending more than 1/3 of your waking hours in your classroom. To have a positive mindset, you need to make sure you utilize this time to your advantage.

Children feed off positive energy; they love to be praised. Use your day to bring positivity to your life and also to all of the children entrusted to your care.

Here are some ideas to get you started:
- Teach your kids positive words and affirmations.
- Post positive notes around your classroom.
- Have a dream board posted in your classroom for the children to put up photos of dreams they have.
- Have the children take turns saying something nice about each of the other children in the class.
- Smile a lot!
- Place incredible value on the children in your eyes.

> *Children feed off positive energy; they love to be praised.*

The positivity in the classroom is as much for the children as it is for you. Posting your goals and dreams on your own wall is important, as well as having classroom goals and dreams. It is never too early to start teaching the children to be more positive. You will be changing lives!

Remember this important gem

for having an amazing mindset: **Have a positive classroom.**

Gem #47

Beware of Your Circle of Influence

"You need to associate with people that inspire you, people that challenge you to rise higher, people that make you better. Don't waste your valuable time with people that are not adding to your growth. Your destiny is too important."

~ Joel Osteen

Working in the child care business is amazing, and it is a huge responsibility. You work in a setting where you are molding young, impressionable minds based on your teaching, attitude, and actions.

Beware of your circle of influence. More than likely you have friends in and out of the child care business. We want to break them down into two different areas for discussion.

You have a job far more important than any other job, don't you forget it!

Friends outside of your center: These may be people you have known before you were a teacher. This could include high school or college friends, roommates or even relatives.

These people can't picture you as a teacher, influencing young minds and changing the world. They may see you like a babysitter and not value what you do for a profession. Beware of this circle of influence because they can put you down and pressure you into changing your career. We have seen it many times.

Remember this always: if a friend does not support your career choice, you need to find a different friend. You have a job far more important than any other job, don't you forget it!

So be the leader in your circle of influence outside of your center. You be the positive one and help to bring your friends to your level. If they fail to come to you, replace them in your circle of influence or we can promise you will end up just like them.

Friends inside your center: This group is made up of like-minded people who are on a mission to make a difference in the world. Your friends here respect what you do, but not everyone here is a positive person. Some may gossip about others behind their backs, others may not be pulling their weight at the center.

You need to be the leader here and influence those in your center for the positive. Use the techniques in this book to raise the bar at your school. Positivity in your life is important; positivity at your school is vital. Work hard at creating a culture of excellence and you will quickly get promoted within your school. Every owner loves a leader who influences others in the school towards positive change.

So to recap, be careful who you hang around with. If you are going to hang around people without your values, work hard to influence them to your way of thinking. If you cannot, replace them quickly with positive friends. Your life will quickly become happier by doing so.

Remember this important gem for having an amazing mindset: **Beware of your circle of influence.**

Gem #48

A Rising Tide Lifts All Boats

"When we focus on our gratitude, the tide of disappointment goes out and the tide of love rushes in."

~ Kristin Armstrong

As the old story goes, a chain is only as strong as its weakest link. A chain is made up of dozens, and sometimes hundreds of links. They are circular pieces of metal that are attached through a hole in the chain. A chain can be used for only one purpose, to pull in one direction or the other. It is worthless without stress and pressure being applied to the chain as a whole.

As tension increases and stresses are applied to the chain it will start to stretch out until it reaches the point where the link of the chain that can't stand the pressure fails. Thus, a chain is only as strong as its weakest link.

A child care team is only as strong as its weakest team member.

A child care team is only as strong as its weakest team member. As a leader in the child care industry, you need to be vigilant about protecting your attitude and actions at all times to continue to be part of a strong team.

If you see weakness in your team, work with that person to help them get stronger so you can all continue to be stronger. We don't care if you are an assistant teacher or an assistant director, each job is equally important to the mission of making a difference in the world.

Now as you do your job tomorrow, look for the weak links and help to make them stronger, otherwise, the chain may break and that would not be good for anyone.

Here's another way to look at it. A sea is full of waves, and when you're at the top of your wave you may appear to be riding much higher than a person (or boat) who is at the valley between the waves. People look across the sea of their lives and they celebrate when they're riding the top of the wave. However, if you're at the bottom of the wave because of a temporary setback and you look up to the top, you might see someone who appears to be riding higher than you. Because the sea of life is ridden in waves of abundance and also waves of challenge or setback, we can be jealous of others. We can have a *"lack mindset"* where we see others having more or doing better. We can covet what they have or see finite resources.

But a sea that rises is a sea that lifts all boats, not just the boats riding the wave. The boats across the entire sea are lifted by the rising tide. This is a mindset of abundance, not lack. This is knowing that if you help pitch in to get the sea to rise, it will rise for everyone on this journey with you.

Remember this important gem for having an amazing mindset: **A rising tide lifts all boats.**

Teresa & Jillian's Story

Jillian and Teresa were becoming a stronger and stronger teaching team in the Pre-K classroom. Parents were commenting on how well their children were performing and learning, enrollment was at its all-time peak, and the child behavior issues they had faced were all but gone.

The teachers were chatting one day and Teresa mentioned that her former employer had a Teacher Mentor program. New teachers were paired with seasoned teachers so they had a *"buddy"* to learn from and be mentored by, from day one. Jillian thought it was a fantastic idea! So they brought the idea to Donna's attention and offered to create the program as a pilot.

Three months later, the LeapFrog Teacher Mentor program is in full swing at the school. New hires are on-boarded and given a Mentor that takes them to lunch during their first week and shows them the ropes. The program is laid out with specific deliverables for the first nine months of every new teacher's employment at LeapFrog. This program helps prevent "*weak links*" in the chain of teachers at the school. It also lifts the tide of all boats, as everyone continues to grow and improve professionally as an early childhood educator.

Gem #49

Have a Dream Board

"The vast majority of people are born, grow up, struggle, and go through life in misery and failure, not realizing that it would be just as easy to switch over and get exactly what they want out of life, not recognizing that the mind attracts the thing it dwells upon."

~ Napoleon Hill

When we first learned about the Law of Attraction, we both thought it was a bunch of malarkey. Is it possible you could attract wealth by thinking of wealth? Who can attract good health by thinking of good health? It sounded weird to both of us.

As we started to read Positive Mental Attitude books we both started noticing a common theme, many of the books had a component of using your mind to help you achieve what you want in life.

We both read Napoleon Hill's *Think and Grow Rich*. It is not titled work and grow rich, it is THINK and grow rich.

We also both have read the book *The Secret* by Rhonda Byrne and we knew there must be some validity to this. We both have created dream boards in our lives.

> *Create a dream board, or vision board, and help your children to create their own. It is never too early in life to dream.*

When you put your dreams on a board that you can look at daily, your subconscious brain will work hard to achieve them, regardless of whether you were consciously aware of the action or not.

Create a dream board, or vision board, and help your children to create their own. It is never too early in life to dream. Post your dream board in a place in your home where you can see it every day. Your brain will work hard to help make it a reality for you. Go read some of the books we recommend. Practice positive self-talk, hang around positive people and practice the gems we have written especially for you daily, and you too can have everything in life your heart desires.

Remember this important gem for having an amazing mindset: **Have a dream board.**

Teresa & Jillian's Story

Earlier, you read about Teresa's vision board or dream board, and how inspired she was to make her dream of an Italy trip come true. They also implemented the idea to share the project with all the teachers at LeapFrog, and every teacher, as well as admin staff, now have a dream board posted in a prominent place at home. They took photos of each board and posted them in a montage in the staff break room, so everyone's dreams could be encouraged and nurtured among each other. It was an amazing team-builder that resulted in an even stronger company culture at the school.

Gem #50

Light Someone Else's Candle

"Thousands of candles can be lighted from a single candle, and the life of the candle will not be shortened. Happiness never decreases by being shared."

~ Buddha

Have you ever been to a candlelight church service? It is a pretty amazing experience if you have never done it. The room is darkened as the story of how Jesus, one by one, found his Disciples and lit his candle. They, in turn, went out and lit candles one at a time, and before you knew it the whole church was lit with hundreds of candles. All from a single candle who had not suffered one bit for sharing the light.

You have a candle inside of you. The light you have needs to be shared with the world. You are in an amazing profession, one where you make a difference. You light the candles of your children each and every day, all without diminishing your own. You also need to take the happiness candle and light up your friends' lives.

> *The light you have needs to be shared with the world.*

When we come to work and act negatively, we help to extinguish the candles of other people. If you help a positive person's candle to go out, then, just like a candle that blows out it cannot light another.

So, be careful about who you allow to influence you. Be sure to always be a candle lighter, going forth and making the world a better place. If there is someone you know who needs their candle lit, don't be stingy with your light, let it shine for the world to see.

Remember this important gem for having an amazing mindset: **Light someone else's candle.**

Gem #51

Laugh Daily

"The most wasted of all days is one without laughter."

~ E E Cummings

The average infant laughs over 200 times a day, the average adult less than twelve. Did you ever stop and think if they might be laughing at us for not being able to laugh at ourselves?

> *This is why laughter is the best medicine because it is actually medicine! Make a point to laugh every single day.*

They say laughter is the best medicine because it is! When you laugh, you excite the motor region of your brain to become active which produces the physical part of laughter and the vocal part as well. Laughter immediately increases the heart rate and makes the body produce antibodies that help to boost your immune system.

Laughter also decreases stress hormones and increases the release of endorphins, the body's feel-good chemical. This is why laughter is the best medicine because it is actually medicine!

Make a point to laugh every single day. Since you work around children all day, this should not be hard. Find humor in all things and learn to laugh at yourself. When faced with a stressful situation, laugh.

Try to make it a point to spend 30 minutes a day watching something funny, especially at the end of the day. It will help you to relax and get rid of the stress of the day. There is always something stupidly funny on YouTube you can watch on your phone if you need a laugh. Make it a point to try to laugh a lot, especially at the end of the day, and watch your life begin to change.

Remember this important gem for having an amazing mindset: **Laugh daily.**

Gem #52

Don't Let Another Person Steal Your Joy

"I refuse to permit anything or anyone to steal my joy regardless of how dire the circumstance is. Happiness is now a way of living for me because I decided a decade ago that it was time to take charge and become the captain of my own thoughts and beliefs."

~ Edmond Mbiaka

Your joy is the one thing that you want to make sure no one ever takes from you. It is the one thing that you have control over, and to let someone take it from you robs you of the power of choice.

Joy and happiness are a choice. You can choose to live a life of joy and happiness or you can choose a life of misery. We have all seen miserable people; no one wants to be around that person.

On the other hand, everyone wants to be around a joyous person. Think of the happiest person you know, can't you just spend all day with that person? Think of the most miserable person you know, spending 10 minutes with this person is 10 minutes too long!

> *Your joy is the one thing that you want to make sure no one ever takes from you.*

When you let someone else take your joy you are letting them have power over your mindset, which no one should have. You need to have control over your own thoughts.

The next time someone tries to steal your joy, pull out your thankfulness journal and think of all of the things you are thankful for, and stay in a joyous mindset.

If you are a positive person, there are going to be a lot of negative people trying to steal your joy. Your positivity will drive them nuts. Do not give them the power. Use your power to persuade them that a joyous life is a happier life. As the smallest candle will light up the darkest room, a joyous teacher will light up an entire center.

Remember this important gem for having an amazing mindset: **Don't let another person steal your joy.**

Gem #53

Create an Educational Commute

"Education is the most powerful weapon which you can use to change the world."

~Nelson Mandela

Unless you walk to your school each day, more than likely you spend time commuting to and from work. The educational commute is one way to start and end your day in an amazing way.

If you love books and do not really have time to read, consider switching to audiobooks. You will then be able to listen to positive mental attitude books on the way to and from your workplace each day. You will arrive at work with a better mindset, and after a long day of work you can put yourself in a positive mood while you drive home.

What should you listen to? Positive podcasts are excellent. Download them onto your phone and listen to them while you drive. Get a positive book on Audible and listen to it while commuting. If you ask your boss, we bet he or she would let you listen to something positive during naptime.

The educational commute is one way to start and end your day in an amazing way.

In today's busy world we do not have the time we once had to sit and read for hours, but most of us still have to commute. Use that time wisely and you will live a much happier life.

Remember this important gem for having an amazing mindset: **Create an educational commute.**

Gem #54

Be Consistent

"Success isn't always about greatness. It's about consistency. Consistent hard work leads to success. Greatness will come."

~ Dwayne Johnson (The Rock)

It takes 21 days to form a good or bad habit. A habit is a consistent behavior that is repeated often enough that it happens without conscious thought. Think of a bad habit you may have. Do you do it without thinking about it? The answer is yes.

> *You need to create positive consistent actions and repeat them each and every day until they become a habit.*

Consistency forms habits, both good and bad. To make positive changes in your life, you need to create positive consistent actions and repeat them each and every day until they become a habit.

In the book *The Slight Edge*, Jeff Olson shows you how to create daily disciplines that, when repeated consistently over time, will form positive changes in your life.

If you are overweight, the consistent daily discipline of exercise will help you lose weight. If you have a negative mindset, the consistent daily discipline of reading positive books will make you happier. If you have no money in savings, the consistent daily discipline of saving a little bit every day will grow your bank account.

Every goal you have in life can be achieved through consistent disciplines repeated daily over time. Creating these habits will seem so natural that not doing them will feel weird to you.

"You'll never change your life until you change something you do daily. The secret of your success is found in your daily routine."

~ John C. Maxwell

Remember this important gem for having an amazing mindset: **Be consistent.**

Gem #55

Live Significantly

"Success is when I add value to myself. Significance is when I add value to others."

~ John Maxwell

Dr. John C. Maxwell is the #1 seller of leadership and mindset books in the world. A common theme in many of his books is living a life of significance. Significance is when you add value to others through your actions. Living a life of significance is one of the most rewarding things someone can do to live a fulfilling life.

As a teacher, you add value to others each and every day. Your attitude and your actions affect the children you teach as well as your co-workers.

To add value to the children you need to treat every child as if they were your own. Adding value means finding patience when a child gets on your nerves. Adding value means giving a hug when the child is misbehaving. Adding value means greeting every parent with an enthusiastic smile and big hello each morning. Adding value means mentoring a new teacher and making this person feel welcome.

As a teacher, you add value to others each and every day.

There are so many ways you can add value to others in any day, it is a choice. To live a life of significance you must always be on the lookout for ways in which to add value to others. Doing so will make your life that much more fulfilling and enjoyable.

Remember this important gem for having an amazing mindset: **Live significantly.**

Teresa & Jillian's Story

Teresa was familiar with the idea of adding value to others. She regularly volunteered at her children's school and also at the local pet shelter. Volunteering made her feel really good. She was driven to make a difference in the lives of others – from children, to animals, to adults.

She noticed that Jillian seemed to lack this opportunity in her life – the chance to give back to others and add significance to the life of someone (or something) else. Teresa invited Jillian to go with her to the local shelter the following Tuesday night, just to experience how it felt. Jillian agreed but had low expectations. She was unsure of how it would go.

At the end of that Tuesday evening, Jillian was super-charged with energy, enthusiasm, and optimism! She couldn't believe how great she felt – after all, it was just an animal shelter. She enjoyed dogs throughout her life but had never been a huge animal lover. Jillian left the shelter feeling like she had really made a difference. She signed up for a weekly volunteer shift and her life has more meaning.

Both ladies talked to Donna about the possibility of doing a field trip for their Pre-K class to the animal shelter. Donna wholeheartedly agreed and they made it happen, much to the delight of the children!

Gem #56

Jump Out of Bed Every Morning

"When you arise in the morning, think of what a precious privilege it is to be alive, to breathe, to think, to enjoy, to love."

~ *Marcus Aurelius*

If you need coffee to become enthusiastic about your day, you are missing out on life. Caffeine is a drug, a very powerful and addictive drug.

Remember when we told you about consistency. If you are a caffeine addict your brain has become addicted to the drug and it needs it to function. Your brain has convinced you that your world is in slow motion without coffee.

> *Become a happy person, one who is happy no matter what time of day.*

If you are telling us that you cannot function without coffee and could never jump out of bed, let us ask you a question. If your house were on fire could you jump out of bed and perform the act of getting your family out, or do you need to have a cup of coffee first?

"I am just not a morning person." We hear that a lot. 100% of our days have mornings, and they make up half of our waking day. Hating mornings means you are hating half of your life, and that is no way to live.

Become a happy person, one who is happy no matter what time of day. One where you jump out of bed ready to tackle what life has to offer that day. You cannot achieve one goal in life while laying in bed unless your goal is to get bed sores.

It is okay to drink caffeine, in moderation. If you really love coffee jump out of bed and make yourself a cup!

For the next 21 days try jumping out of bed and greeting your day with enthusiasm and appreciation. There are so many things you should be thankful for. Enthusiastically start your day reading and adding to your thankfulness journal and your day will be much more fulfilling.

Remember this important gem for having an amazing mindset: **Jump out of bed every morning.**

Gem #57

Leave Your Ego at the Door

"If someone corrects you and you feel offended, then you have an ego problem."

~ Nouman Ali Khan

Over our many years in this industry, we have both noticed a change in teachers' ability to take constructive feedback and use it to improve their lives. It seems like when an owner tries to give feedback, ego kicks in and the employee immediately gets upset thinking that he or she should not be the subject of much ridicule from the owner.

If this is you, then you have an ego problem. You think you are above constructive feedback and you are better than everyone else. If this is you, please stop it right now. Leave your ego at the door. You do not know everything, no one does. If someone gives you the gift of constructive feedback, say thank you with a huge smile on your face.

Let's say that you have to go from your house to the store,

and have gone the same way for years. You tell a friend that you went to the store and on the way, you witnessed an accident on Carver Street. Your friend asks why didn't you go down Main Street, it is much shorter. You investigate and find out your friend is correct.

Do you get upset when your friend tells you that you were going the long way? Did you have an attitude about it? Hopefully not.

When your supervisor, a friend, your boss, or maybe the kids you are teaching give you some advice, accept it with a thank you. It is a gift meant to help make you better at your job, which is to teach the next generation.

Leave your ego at the door. You do not know everything, no one does.

Remember this important gem for having an amazing mindset: **Leave your ego at the door.**

Gem #58

Take Control of Your Life

"No one is in control of your happiness but you; therefore, you have the power to change anything about yourself or your life that you want to change."

~ Barbara de Angelis

No one has control over your life but you. It is very important to never forget that you have all of the power for your life to turn out exactly how you want it to.

If you want to someday be a millionaire, you can do it.

If you someday want to be a director, you can do it. If you someday want to own a home, you can do it. If you someday want a family, you can do it.

Your past decisions in life have gotten you to the exact point in life you are in right now. You can never blame anyone else for where you are today. When you become an adult you lose the right to blame someone else for where you are in life.

When you become an adult you lose the right to blame someone else for where you are in life.

If you don't like your income, get more education. If you don't like your profession, find a different job. If you don't like your car, save for a new one. If you don't like your home, move. If you don't like the way your boyfriend treats you, find a better one.

You have the power to make your life as good or as bad as you wish, you have all of the power. Stop making excuses for why you are not where you want to be in life. Never play the blame game. Take responsibility for your actions, take control over your life, and write the future you want to live.

Remember this important gem for having an amazing mindset: **Take control of your life.**

Teresa & Jillian's Story

Both Teresa and Jillian started feeling more and more empowered by the personal growth and positive mindset ideas they were reading and being exposed to. They started achieving their goals and accomplishing dreams on their "*bucket lists.*" Jillian had never felt more physically fit and strong in her body and mind. Teresa was just a few months away from her trip to Italy with hubby, Tom, and rarely had a drink. When she did drink, it was an occasional glass of wine as a treat during a night out on the town.

The teachers were operating as an integrated collaborative team in the classroom. While they still had occasional communication issues with parents and behavioral challenges with kids, they could see and feel the difference in mindset and positivity in their daily lives. They also held each other accountable to perform at the highest level possible.

Teresa decided to talk to Donna about the possibility of a bigger leadership position in the organization. During their regular 1-on-1 meetings, Donna helped each teacher identify their path to success and personal growth.

Gem #59

Everyone Needs a Jen in Their Life

"The rise or fall, success or failure of your dreams is largely dependent on the association you build yourself around."

~ Israelmore Ayivor

Brian Duprey & Jen Slavin

From Brian: In my job as a Certified Child Care Coach, I have met hundreds of child care center owners and staff members from around the world. About two years ago, I met an amazing person named Jennifer Slavin. Jen is Vice President of Operations of a chain of nine child care centers in Pennsylvania.

As a positive mindset guru, I naturally gravitate to positive people. Jen is one of the most positive people I have ever met in my life. Her attitude, for such a young person, is a testimony of how she was brought up. She reminds me of my own daughters, and we quickly became friends. She speaks of her Dad often to me, and how amazing he is. It is rare for such a young person to have such an incredible mindset. I credit her parents and her upbringing.

Everyone needs a Jen, someone that can light up any darkness in your life with a smile, a text, a call, a hug or an email. Make sure when you find your Jen you do the same for that person, and together you can be a positive force for good in the world. Agree to always try to outdo each other on the positivity front and I promise you, your life will change for the better.

From Kris: We chose Jen to receive the 2018 Director of the Year award at our annual Child Care Success Summit conference (www.childcaresuccesssummit.com). It goes to show you that a positive mindset will help you get promoted, advanced, and recognized in your job. There is a reason positive people make more money and get promoted much faster than negative people. It pays to be positive; plus it feels a whole lot better!

Jen's positivity has had a huge impact on the success and growth of her company and her team. Her leadership helps retain teachers and keep them engaged and motivated. Her owner Neydary has been able to count on Jen's leadership as Executive Director, enabling them to expand together from 3 to 9 locations in just one year. Jen's impact is felt through the trickle-down effect of teachers to parents to children.

Remember this important gem for having an amazing mindset: **Everyone needs a Jen in their life.** And maybe even more important, *how can YOU be a Jen?*

Gem #60

Don't Be Afraid to Ask For Help

"The only mistake you can make is not asking for help."

~ Sandeep Jauhar

One of the biggest mistakes a teacher can make, especially a new teacher, is not asking for help. There are times when you need a mental health break from the children, especially if you have difficult children to teach.

If you find yourself losing patience and getting frustrated, please ask your director for help. Seek guidance on teaching methods that may help the situation, and also get some time away from the classroom when you are at your wit's end.

Asking for help is not a sign of weakness but a sign of strength.

The last thing you want to do is lose your temper in the classroom; this could cost you your job. Do not be afraid to ask for help when you find yourself getting to that point.

If you are a new teacher, or new to the program, be sure to know who you can go to for questions and to get help. Hopefully, your school has a mentorship program where there is mentoring of new teachers by seasoned veterans.

If you are having problems at home, you also need to ask for help. As a teacher, it is not fair to the children to bring your personal problems to work, but, if you find that this is happening, please ask for help.

We have spoken to some owners who told us that they have had teachers in abusive relationships at home that were stalked and harassed at school. They asked for help and were helped by their owners. Others have had teachers with substance abuse issues that have asked for help, and they were able to help them.

Asking for help is not a sign of weakness but a sign of strength. You are strong enough to know that you cannot get through the situation by yourself. Talk to your director and owner and keep them notified of situations that may affect your work performance and seek help when you need it.

Remember this important gem for having an amazing mindset: **Don't be afraid to ask for help.**

Gem #61

Get Out of Your Comfort Zone

"You have to get outside of your comfort zone if you're going to make significant changes in your life, and since few things scare people like the unknown, feeling fear is an excellent sign that you're on the right track."

~ Jen Sincero

From Brian: In 2003, I did something crazy, I jumped out of an airplane from 10,500 feet. I did it because my daughter, Aubrey, was afraid of heights. I have always taught my children to face their fears head-on and live life outside of their comfort zone.

My wife is not afraid of anything, so she volunteered to go first. I stayed on the ground praying that I would not witness a giant splat on the ground in front of me. I watched as she jumped out of the plane with her instructor in a tandem jump. As I watched the parachute open a sigh of relief came over me as I watched her slowly sail to the ground.

Next, it was Aubrey's turn. She and I got up to 10,500 feet

and I watched as fear engulfed her face. As the plane door opened she tried to grab the door to keep herself inside the plane. The instructor calmly tucked her arms to her side and jumped out of the plane while I watched.

After we landed, I went over and asked her how she liked it and she said she had loved it. I had cured her of her fear of heights because action cures fear and one of the best things you can do in life is live outside of your comfort zone.

Action cures fear and one of the best things you can do in life is live outside of your comfort zone.

After my wife and daughter went, it was then my turn. I was very scared, more than I have ever been in my life. Having them go first and then me back out would have sent a very hypocritical message to my daughter, so I did the jump. It was uncomfortable but simply amazing.

What are you afraid to do? What makes you uncomfortable? What do you fear? There are so many things in the world that exist outside of your comfort zone, but those things are extremely rewarding. Think back to a time when you did something you were uncomfortable doing, was it worth it afterward?

Action cures fear. Make a commitment today to do something in the next 30 days that is outside of your comfort zone. We can promise you, life truly begins when you are not afraid to push the boundaries of your comfort level.

Remember this important gem for having an amazing mindset: **Get outside of your comfort zone.**

Gem #62

Accept Change as a Good Thing

"Change the changeable, accept the unchangeable, and remove yourself from the unacceptable."

~ Denis Waitley

As child care coaches, we have a unique vantage point when we coach a client. We can see things that they cannot see. When you are a teacher, you can often see potential in a child that they do not see in themselves yet.

Change is a good thing, not a bad thing.

Change is a good thing, not a bad thing. You are part of a child care center team and that team performs best when all of the team members are in the right seats. Your owner may ask you to teach toddlers instead of preschool. She may ask you to transfer to another location. She may ask you to take on more responsibility by acting as an assistant director.

Take it as a compliment when asked to take on new challenges and responsibilities. If your owner has faith and confidence in you, they more than likely can see things that you do not see. Accept change as a good thing and work hard at whatever you are asked to do.

Occasionally owners have to change things. Working hours may have to be adjusted, classrooms may have to be consolidated, software programs may be changed, policies may vary, employee benefits may be added or removed.

Take each change with a positive attitude, remember you do not know all of the facts as to why the change was necessary. Owners have to make decisions every day knowing that if they make the wrong one they could lose everything, so please cut them some slack when change is asked for. Know in your heart they would not do it unless they deemed it absolutely necessary.

Remember this important gem for having an amazing mindset: **Accept change as a good thing.**

Teresa & Jillian's Story

Teresa had realized over her years of being a teacher that she was drawn to change. She seemed to get bored with routine, especially after about a four year period. She liked to switch up the classroom design and décor on a regular basis, and most of the children in her class responded to change well.

On the other hand, Jillian was averse to change. She liked the status quo and being safely inside her comfort zone 'bubble'. Whenever Teresa suggested a change to the classroom layout, she got quite nervous and even anxious. This difference in comfort level with change caused friction between the two women.

After reading this gem, Teresa had a huge insight into her friend and colleague! She took the time to sit down with Jillian and have a heart to heart chat about their differences. Teresa assured Jillian that she would not make changes without consulting her and giving her plenty of input in any changes prior to executing them.

Gem #63

Deal Positively with Negative Co-Workers

"Stop letting people who do so little for you control so much of your mind, feelings, and emotions."

~ Will Smith

You are probably noticing a common thing in this book: who you hang around with matters. Unfortunately, most of the time we cannot pick our co-workers and sometimes you must work around Negative Nellie's.

We have written this book to change your life. Embrace it and go forth and have an amazing life.

A Negative Nellie will always ruin your day if you let her. She complains about everything and is unhappy with the world around her. No one wants to be around her, yet she has many friends. Remember the old saying, birds of a feather flock together?

Negative Nellie's hate positive and will naturally repel anything positive you try to introduce, at first. It takes time to turn a Negative Nellie into a Positive Pamela. Sometimes it takes years. Be the most positive person at all times around her and when she sees how happy you are at your life, eventually she will want to take a run at happiness herself.

Convince her to read this book and pay particular attention to the chapter on mindset. We cannot look into someone's brain and see their upbringing. Maybe she was an abused child, maybe she suffered a traumatic incident in her life, maybe no one ever showed her how to be positive.

Since we cannot see into someone's past, we should not judge the person for the behavior. We should love them and do our best to help them see that a positive life beats a negative life.

If you are reading this gem and you do not know any negative people, then you might be the Negative Nellie. We have written this book to change your life. Embrace it and go forth and have an amazing life.

Remember this important gem for having an amazing mindset: **Deal positively with negative co-workers.**

Gem #64

Remember the Ten-Thousand-Hour Rule

"Experience is a hard teacher because she gives the test first, the lesson afterward."

~ *Vernon Law*

Remember the first time you tried to ride a bike, you fell. What about the first time you tried to ice skate or ski? We bet you fell a lot!

We learn from experience and time. The longer we do something the better we get at it. We must program our brain and muscles through what is called muscle memory.

How does a professional basketball player sink a 3-point shot consistently? Muscle memory. How does a professional baseball player throw a baseball 100 miles an hour in the same

> *It takes 10,000 hours to become a master at something.*

spot every time? Muscle memory.

The same way professional athletes train is the same way you will become an amazing teacher.

It takes 10,000 hours to become a master at something. If you work 40 hours a week, that means in five years you will become a master at it.

Don't beat yourself up if you aren't the best teacher after your first year or two, it takes time. Experience is a great teacher and it helps you to develop confidence as well. Give yourself a break the next time you are frustrated with not doing everything to perfection (your idea of perfection). Practice makes perfect and you may have a few thousand hours to go until you are there.

Remember this important gem for having an amazing mindset: **Remember the ten-thousand-hour rule.**

Chapter 4 Notes:

_____

_____

_____

_____

_____

_____

_____

_____

_____

_____

_____

_____

_____

_____

_____

_____

_____

_____

Chapter 5

Leadership

"A leader's job is not to do the work for others, it's to help others figure out how to do it themselves, to get things done, and to succeed beyond what they thought possible."

~ Simon Sinek

lead·er·ship · noun

1. The action of leading a group of people or an organization.

You may be thinking, *"I am not a leader."* If you are thinking that, you are wrong. Each day you are tasked with jobs that require leadership. Owners lead an entire team. Directors lead staff. Head teachers lead assistant teachers. Teachers lead children and parents as well.

Everyone leads someone or is being led by someone else, and the more you know about leadership, the easier it will be to be able to be a more effective leader.

"Leadership is not about titles, positions or flowcharts. It is about one life influencing another."

~ John C. Maxwell

Think about this quote for a moment. People do not follow titles, they follow someone they respect and they allow that person to have influence over them.

As a leader, you set the tone for an entire organization. *"The leader's attitude is like a thermostat for the place she works. If her attitude is good, the atmosphere is pleasant, and the environment is easy to work in. But if her attitude is bad, the temperature is insufferable." ~ John C. Maxwell*

Leadership is not bossing people around. You cannot make anyone do anything and if you are using threats to get someone to do something, you are not leading; you are forcing them against their will and it will always backfire on you.

Leadership is respect. How you treat the leader above you will be in direct proportion to how you will be treated as a leader. If you want respect, you must show and give respect.

Very few people are natural leaders. We have placed our leadership book recommendations at the end of the book. If you want to be a better leader you must learn to be a better follower. Start reading some books and you will be well on your way to grow as a person. We have written this chapter for the leaders of the center, in which we consider everyone to lead someone. Some of the gems apply more to directors and head teachers, but they are important for all to read regardless of your position. If today is your first day and you have no education or qualifications, there is no reason you cannot work to become the director of a school in only a few years.

This is a great profession for advancement. If you get educated, you can rise fast and advance to be a director or an assistant director in only a few years and your salary will increase. You will also have a chance to make a bigger impact on the planet by having the power to influence change. We believe in you and we hope now after reading this book you believe in yourself.

"The younger you are, the more likely you will give your attention to many things. That's good because if you're young you're still getting to know yourself, your strengths and weaknesses. If you focus your thinking

on only one thing and your aspirations change, then you've wasted your best mental energy. As you get older and more experienced, the need to focus becomes more critical. The farther and higher you go, the more focused you can be—and need to be."

~ John C. Maxwell

Gem #65

Recognition is Important

"Don't work for recognition, but do work worthy of recognition."

~ H. Jackson Brown, Jr.

As a leader, it is important for you to recognize others for their accomplishments. Everyone craves recognition in some fashion and finding how to properly recognize someone is key to being able to effectively lead them.

> *Everyone craves recognition, but few know how to give it properly.*

Recognition is very important to overall company morale. If you are only working for recognition, and fail to get recognized, it will dampen your attitude. If you do work worthy of recognition and do not get it, you can still be proud that you did the work to the best of your ability and, since cream always rises to the top, recognition will naturally come.

Be sure to recognize those who report to you for showing initiative and doing great work. Recognition can be as little as a sincere thank you to a handwritten card to something more elaborate like a gift card. Always know the best way to reward excellent work and you will notice that the person will continue this excellent behavior. Everyone craves recognition, but few know how to give it properly.

Don't be afraid to ask someone how they like to be recognized. Ask them what their favorite hot beverage is and bring it to them with a thank you card. Get them a gift card to their favorite restaurant. Find what motivates each person and tailor it specifically to them and you will improve your staff culture and have a staff want to work hard for you.

Remember this important gem on leadership: **Recognition is important.**

Gem #66

There is Power in a Name

"A person's name is to him or her the sweetest and most important sound in any language."

~ Dale Carnegie

Have you ever been introduced to someone and three seconds after they tell you their name you have forgotten it? Have you ever driven right by the exit you were supposed to get off of? Have you ever walked into a room and you forgot what you went into the room for? It has to do with how our brains are wired.

Memories are tricky and, the more we can make connections in the brain, the easier it is to remember things. Names are one of the hardest things to remember but with a few suggestions, you will be remembering a lot better.

A person's name is the sweetest sound in the world to them. Nothing makes a person feel more special than remembering their name and repeating it back to them upon meeting again.

When you meet someone new, try to associate that person with some other memory in your life. If you were to meet Sally Fish, maybe you remember a time you went fishing and had a good laugh, so it was a silly fishing trip. So when you see Sally's face, it reminds you of a silly fishing trip and your brain can recall the name, Sally Fish. Salespeople also have a trick of repeating a person's name back to them several times in the first few minutes of a meeting.

A person's name is the sweetest sound in the world to them.

When you meet Ben White you may think about Big Ben being painted white. Putting a picture image in your mind associated with a name makes it much easier to remember.

When you meet a new teacher, try to make it a point to remember this person's name. Repeat it back to them often and they will appreciate you so very much for it.

Use this technique with anything you need to remember: dates, appointments, hotel room numbers, parking garage levels. Make connections in your brain with past memories and you will be the envy of all of your friends with the incredible memory you will have, but remembering a name is the one that is the most important. Your name is the sweetest sound to you when you hear it.

Remember this important gem on leadership: **There is power in a name.**

Teresa & Jillian's Story

As a mom herself, Teresa had firsthand experience with the joy of hearing the names of her children. There was no subject she loved talking about more than her two children, Taylor and Jennifer. To support that idea, Donna had given the entire staff an enlightening training on enrollment techniques, and one key element of what they learned was personalization. That is, ways to integrate parent's names and children's names into conversation – how to address them, greet them, and build relationships with them.

Teresa was a morning person and had the responsibility of opening the center in the morning. A couple months' prior, Donna realized the need for covering the inbound center phone between opening at 6:30 am and 8:30 am (when she arrived). In addition to opening the building, Teresa was the designated phone coverage person during those hours. Donna trained Teresa to use a modified *"short phone script"* to get the information of parents who may be inquiring to enroll. Part of that script was asking for a bit of caller information, starting with the caller's name and their child's name. This personalized the phone call, and Teresa used the script effectively, to build trust and rapport with each prospective parent. She didn't get a lot of calls early in the morning, but when she did, she was able to do a great job scheduling a tour and building rapport with them. She also used the go-to line *"tell me more about your child"* which worked great to open up a meaningful conversation with the parent on the other line.

Gem #67

Think Before Speaking

"You are master of what you say until you utter it, once you deliver it, you are its captive. Preserve your tongue as you do your gold and money. One word could bring disgrace and the termination of a bliss."

~ *Ali Ibn Abi Talib A.S*

When was the last time you said something you regret? We have all done it, said something you wish you could take back. As a leader, you need to think before you speak. There is a reason God gave us two ears and one mouth, so we will do twice as much listening as we do talking.

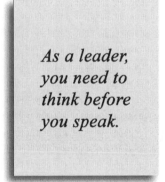

As a leader, you need to think before you speak.

When a teacher comes to you with a problem, really think hard about your response. It is okay to tell someone you will get back to them when asked to solve an issue. It is best to listen to the issue and make sure you consider the consequences of your decision and actions on all parties. A true leader also gets all of the facts first before a decision is made and a response is given.

Remember this gem when you want to comment on someone else's social media post, think before commenting. Taking the extra time to really think before responding will keep you from saying something you may regret later.

Remember this important gem on leadership: **Think before speaking.**

Gem #68

Listen - Not to Respond

"Most people do not listen with the intent to understand; they listen with the intent to reply."

~ *Stephen R. Covey*

Most of us prefer to talk and very few of us like to listen. When we are in a conversation with someone most of us are so busy thinking of the next thing we want to say and are waiting for a pause in the conversation to start talking. Doing so means we are not listening to what other people are saying because we are thinking of the next thing we want to say.

It is important for a leader to be a great listener. Listening is a skill that does not come naturally but most of us can be taught very easily. The easiest way to become a good listener is to genuinely start caring for people. When you take your eyes off yourself and put them on others, you allow yourself to want to hear and understand others.

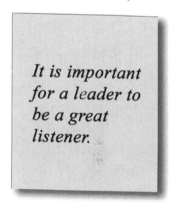

It is important for a leader to be a great listener.

Some tips to help you become a better listener:

* Lean in when someone is speaking to let them know you want to be close enough so you can hear them.
* Ask clarifying questions. Since most people listen to respond, when you listen and ask a question about what is said, it lets the person speaking know you hear them

and care about what they are saying.

- Repeat what is spoken to you back to them to ensure you hear it exactly as they said it.

Remember this important gem on leadership: **Listen - not to respond.**

Gem #69

Mentor Impressionable Teachers

"One of the greatest values of mentors is the ability to see ahead what others cannot see and to help them navigate a course to their destination."

~ *John C. Maxwell*

Anyone that is hired after you is someone you can mentor. Just because you are new yourself does not mean you cannot lead someone else through mentorship.

> *As teachers, we need to be continually learning and striving for advancement.*

Mentorship means taking someone under your wing and training them in areas such as company policies and procedures. In the Child Care Success Academy, we teach our clients to have a mentorship program at your school. Each new teacher is assigned a mentor who will be their go-to person whenever they have a question about anything.

As teachers, we need to be continually learning and striving for advancement. Maybe you are an assistant or substitute teacher and want to be a teacher. Maybe you are a teacher and you want to be an assistant director. Maybe you are an assistant director and you wish to become a director. Whatever you are striving for, find someone who does that role and ask them to mentor you. They will feel honored that you want them to teach you, and your owner will love the fact that you wish to advance in the company.

If your center does not have a mentorship program, we would recommend that you ask your owner or director to create one. You will quickly notice increased teacher retention as your teachers feel more connected from day one.

Remember this important gem on leadership: **Mentor impressionable teachers.**

Gem #70

Properly Onboard a New Teacher

"Tell me and I forget, teach me and I may remember, involve me and I learn."

~ Benjamin Franklin

One of the biggest mistakes a center makes is the improper onboarding of a new employee. Onboarding includes learning all of the center's rules and regulations, background checks, state regulation review, uniform policies, pay and benefits, training requirements and a whole lot more.

The ball is dropped when the employee has signed all of the paperwork, passed the background checks, and is ready to start work. Most owners throw a teacher into the classroom and wish them the best and wonder why our industry turnover is over 30% annually.

If you are a director or an owner we highly recommend reading the book *Relationship Roadmap: Real-World*

> *One of the biggest mistakes a center makes is the improper onboarding of a new employee.*

Strategies for Building a Positive, Collaborative Culture in Your Preschool by Sindye Alexander (available on Amazon). It has amazing strategies on how to properly onboard a new staff member.

If you are not a director or owner, maybe someday you will be. The more you learn now, the easier it will be for you to transition to this role in the future. As a leader, you have to ensure that all new teachers are properly on boarded and that they have continual ongoing training and support and that they feel appreciated.

Remember this important gem on leadership: **Properly onboard a new teacher.**

Gem #71

Keep Your Distance

"Leaders must be close enough to relate to others, but far enough ahead to motivate them."

~ *John C. Maxwell*

One of the hardest leadership lessons for a new leader to learn is when to be a friend and when to be a leader. Most directors at child care centers are former teachers and many of them are now leading teachers that they used to work side by side with.

Those who work for you are not your friends in the traditional sense of the word, they work for you and there is an employee/boss relationship. You, of course, can be friendly, but the more you blur the lines of leadership, the more issues you will have at leading them.

If you were a close friend and equal co-worker with someone and you now lead them, there might be an expectation of favoritism. You need to learn to keep your distance and be sure to set clear boundaries so the lines do not blur.

A leader should be setting the example on and off the clock.

Keeping your distance means not hanging out one on one in your off time. A leader should be setting the example on and off the clock. If a subordinate sees a leader making questionable decisions or acting foolishly at a bar, for example, it will reduce the effectiveness of leading them at work.

If you hang out with selective staff members and everyone is not invited, it will lower the morale of the whole center. Staff members will see the person you are hanging around with as being a favorite and receiving special treatment causing gossiping to happen behind your back.

This does not mean you cannot ever see them in your off time, quite the contrary. It is perfectly fine to arrange an outing with your staff but ensure that everyone is invited. Go bowling, to a movie, have a cookout, maybe a mani/pedi or spa day for all team members. No one will feel left out if everyone is invited.

Leading former close friends is a very tough job, you will feel very isolated and alone. You will see workers talking behind your back and more than likely about you. Leadership is about influence and respect, and you will garnish more by keeping the leadership lines clear than by blurring them and coming down to their level.

Remember this important gem on leadership: **Keep your distance.**

Gem #72

Eliminate Gossip

"People who judge harshly, criticize and condemn others through gossip, rumor or bad word of mouth are setting themselves up for the same unfair trials."

~ Scott Allan

There is nothing more disastrous to a child care center culture than rampant gossip running through the school. Avoiding some of the things we write about in this book will help, but repetitive training on this subject will help to keep it in check as much as possible.

> *A good leader never talks badly about anyone behind his or her back.*

A good leader never talks badly about anyone behind his or her back. This includes parents, employees, competitors or vendors. The reason is simple: if you are heard spreading gossip about someone, that person you are speaking to will assume you do the same thing about them when they are not around.

We both have heard many times in the child care business that, because it is a mostly female workforce, gossiping is inevitable. But you, as the leader, are the key. You must be a role model for eliminating gossip, both by NOT engaging in it, and by constantly reinforcing a *"no gossip zone"* in your center.

In today's social media world, there is so much that we know about people that many of us find it impossible to not want to talk about others. We see social media posts that always show a person's positive side, often hiding the truth. By knowing so much about other people, we have become a nation of nosey people, prying into other people's lives and watching the soap opera of other's lives airing out in your news feed.

Assume everything you read on the internet is fabricated, photoshopped, and only a glimmer of truth and you will be better off. Resist commenting and liking others posts because doing so is injecting your opinion into their world, which makes it much easier to gossip.

Leaders should never comment on social media posts of the people that they lead. You may think that when someone posts something on their newsfeed that they are inviting feedback, but that is often not the case. Most who post are looking for affirmation that they are doing the right thing, and anything that is contrary to that would be unwelcomed and could hurt you as their leader.

Remember this important gem on leadership: **Eliminate gossip.**

Teresa & Jillian's Story

One of Donna's core leadership goals at Leapfrog Preschool was maintaining it as a *"no-gossip zone."* All new employees were on boarded to the policy and culture of *"lifting each other up"* and not engaging in workplace gossip. But as human nature tends to go, it sometimes proved very difficult for teachers not to gossip with each other. Because teacher teams were typically segregated by classroom with little cross-class interaction throughout the day, gossip was a natural tendency that was hard to fight.

Teresa and Jillian were no different. While they focused on the children and creatively taught the curriculum throughout the day, sometimes it was hard not to gossip. One of the fun parts of the job was to chit-chat about the personal lives of other staff, when children were napping or on the playground. They didn't mean any harm or to hurt the feelings of another colleague.

One day, the three's teacher named Sara overheard Jillian and Teresa gossiping about the other three's teacher Vivian. Sara rushed back to her classroom to tell Vivian what she overheard – that Vivian's husband was having an affair and their marriage was in big trouble. The gossip was extremely hurtful to Vivian, especially since it was completely untrue! Donna had a huge situation on her hands as the leader. She called Jillian and Teresa into her office and had to write up a Corrective Action Plan for them both, since they broke an important school policy.

Jillian and Teresa felt awful. They doubled down on their efforts to avoid gossip at all costs, promised to increase their awareness around it, and vowed to hold each other accountable. They had learned a difficult but valuable lesson.

Gem #73

Perfection is an Impossible Standard

"The closest to perfection people ever come is when they write their resumes ."

~ John C. Maxwell

One of the biggest problems we both see when working with owners and directors is many of them are perfectionists. Perfection is impossible and is a very subjective standard and very much in the eye of the beholder.

One person's idea of perfection will be far different from another person's, and for the perfectionist that is a hard thing to accept. A perfectionist sees things as *their way* is a perfect way, and that all other ways are unacceptable.

We have seen many owners who drive great directors away by setting impossible standards. We have also seen many directors drive great teachers away by doing the same.

We have also seen leaders who do everything themselves without delegating anything. By delegating important responsibilities to others, you elevate them and allow them to accomplish great things, more than likely even better than you would have done.

So imagine you are climbing a vine on the side of a hill and either one of us is your coach. We tell you to let go of the vine and you are scared. You are afraid you will fall. We say to you to let go, and you do, and there is a net there to catch you.

As your coach, we are asking you to trust us. Let go of the vine and delegate some things off your plate and trust your people. Things do not have to be perfectly done to your satisfaction, they have to be done to their definition of perfection and if that is within 80% of yours, that has to be enough.

We have seen many owners who drive great directors away by setting impossible standards.

You may have to bite your tongue at first. Allow the leader below you to make mistakes, which is the hardest thing for a perfectionist to learn. When we teach our children to ride a bike we accept that falling is a way for them to learn, and mistakes are important to riding excellence.

The same holds true for leadership. Leaders learn from mistakes and we must allow them to be made or frustration will set in and working for you will become impossible for anyone. If you are an owner and you have gone through multiple directors, you may need to look in the mirror and see if you are the problem.

Remember this important gem on leadership: **Perfection is an impossible standard.**

Gem #74

Shield Your Team From Negativity

"You cannot have a positive life and a negative mind."

~ Joyce Meyer

Most of us think that when a baby is born they are naturally positive and are born with a smiling personality. Picture a baby and how often they smile. The reason they smile so much is that everyone who looks at them smiles. There is nothing that can put a smile on your face as much as looking at a tiny little baby. The infant smiles at you because they are learning to imitate you.

> *As a leader, you need to shield your team from as much negative as possible, mostly by accentuating the positive in everything you do.*

The same holds true for leadership, the team members below you will model your actions. If you are a grumpy and negative leader, you will have a grumpy and negative workforce. If you are a positive and happy leader, you will develop a positive and happy workforce.

As a leader, you need to shield your team from as much negative as possible, mostly by accentuating the positive in everything you do. A leader who always looks on the bright side and always sees the best in people will have people willing to follow them. Most people naturally want to be around someone who is a glass half-full type of person.

Unfortunately, there are some Negative Nellie's out there that are not salvageable. These are teachers who suck the energy out of a room and are negative about everything. A teacher who is a Negative Nellie is cancer to a center and that cancer needs to be cut out or it can affect the whole school.

As a leader, you will need to keep negativity from your team. If the center is struggling financially, the teachers do not need to know this. Any uncertainty in their future with you and they will start looking at bailing on you.

Be careful not to criticize your subordinates in front of other people. Always give negative feedback in private. On the other hand, praise should never be done privately and should always be done publicly, for the world to see.

Spend the majority of your time focusing on positive things you can do to improve your center. Place positive sayings around your school, especially at the place where they clock in each day. Turning your school into one that is a positive place to work will take some time, but in the end, you will have increased teacher retention and morale will skyrocket.

Remember this important gem on leadership: **Shield your team from negativity.**

Gem #75

Be a Leader, Not a Boss.

"To lead any way other than by example, we send a fuzzy picture of leadership to others. If we work on improving ourselves first and make that our primary mission, then others are more likely to follow."

~ *John C. Maxwell*

> *There is a huge difference between a boss and a leader.*

There is a huge difference between a boss and a leader. We have seen this mistake made a lot at child care centers.

Here are some of the main differences:

- A boss says go, a leader says let's go.
- A boss points out weaknesses, a leader praises strengths.
- A boss blames others, a leader accepts responsibility.
- A boss demands results, a leader inspires performance.
- A boss focuses on herself, a leader focuses on the team.
- A boss directs, a leader coaches.
- A boss uses people, a leader develops people.
- A boss inspires fear, a leader generates enthusiasm.
- A boss says "*I,*" a leader says "*we.*"
- A boss knows how, a leader shows how.
- A boss takes credit, a leader gives credit.
- A boss talks more than she listens, a leader listens much more than she talks.
- A boss commands, a leader asks.

"People ask the difference between a leader and a boss. The leader leads and the boss drives."

~ Theodore Roosevelt.

Remember this important gem on leadership: **Be a leader, not a boss.**

Gem #76

Time Management is Vital

"Time is what we want most, but what we use worst."

~ William Penn

Time is a commodity that no one has enough of yet we all have the same amount of. Does it drive you crazy when some people seem to be able to get a lot done and others seem to struggle with time management?

Child care center managers are notorious for always being in crisis management mode and time has a way of getting away from them. Each day when an owner or director comes to a center, he or she will face challenges that were not anticipated, and if not managed correctly, will waste an entire day.

> *Time is a commodity that no one has enough of yet we all have the same amount of.*

If you are a teacher you must manage your time wisely to ensure that the children have a schedule that is consistent and reliable. Surprise inspections, bad weather, and staff shortages all have a way of throwing off a teacher's schedule. A good teacher will be consistent in her routine.

Here are some tips for owners and directors to be able to manage time properly. If you are a teacher and you see your director or owner using these methods, learn from them and respect them. One day you may very likely be in the director's chair if you want increased responsibility and pay.

One of the best time management techniques is time blocking. Taking a certain time each day and blocking it out as to not be disturbed for anything other than a bona fide emergency. We recommend getting a stop sign, red means emergency only, do not disturb. Yellow means you can be disturbed for high priority issues and green will mean you are free to be interrupted.

A director or owner will get more done in two uninterrupted hours than she will in a whole day without time blocking. Constant interruptions are a major time suck and keep you from getting into a groove and things will take a task 4-5 times longer to complete.

Block two hours a day (we recommend nap time, this is normally the most quiet time at a center anyway) and give the phone to one of your staff members and put a red light outside of your office. You will quickly notice that you now have your life back. You will be able to leave on time and not have to work weekends just to get the paperwork done.

Another thing about time management that you need to be aware of is Parkinson's Law. *"Work expands so as to fill the time available for its completion."* If you have all day to get three certain things done, more than likely it will take you all day to get those three things done. If you have two hours to do the exact same three things, you will get them done in two hours.

The secret is to have a very long to-do list and try to put two times as many things on your list as a reasonable person could accomplish in a day. You will want to work on the highest priority items first and check them off your list as they get done. Do not wait for deadlines either. If you know payroll has to be processed by Wednesday at 1 pm, do not wait until Wednesday morning to get it done. Plan on having it done Monday, then, if licensing shows up on Tuesday or Wednesday, you are not scrambling. Never work on a project near a deadline, it will cause you the most stress.

We consider this one of the most important gems in this book, one that if you master will change your whole life. Managing time is one of those things that help you to feel like you are cheating in life, allowing yourself what seems like more time in your day.

Remember this important gem on leadership: **Time management is vital.**

Teresa & Jillian's Story

Like many early childhood leaders, Donna struggled with time management. She had so many demands on her time during a typical day running the school. After she took a time management training from Kris Murray, Donna implemented three key ideas that made a huge difference for her.

First, she adopted the time blocking technique and found coverage to get out of the school a couple mornings each week, from 9:30-11:30 am. On Tuesday and Thursday during those times, she went to a coffee shop with one or two projects under her arm. She was able to put on headphones and dive into the projects, completing them with focused time free of interruptions. This was a game changer for Donna!

Second, she wrote her daily schedule on a small portable whiteboard and displayed it through the glass window of her office which faced the school's main corridor and entry way. She tried to display *free time* every day during nap time (usually 1-1:30 pm) when she had Open Office Hours. This allowed her staff to come in every day during a scheduled time rather than interrupt her throughout the day. Again, a huge win!

Finally, she scheduled regular one-on-one meetings with her team each month. Every teacher was scheduled for a 20-minute private meeting with Donna, each month. Just knowing that they would have this time was a great cultural improvement for Donna's teaching team. Staff were asked to "*save up*" a list of things to cover in the one-on-one, if possible, rather than attempt to have one-off conversations. Donna wanted to find a way to do these twice a month because they were so powerful for her leadership success.

Gem #77

Continually Train Future Leaders

"A leader who produces other leaders multiplies their influences."

~ *John C. Maxwell*

If you are an owner, you need to always have leaders trained to run things should something happen to you or your director. If you are a director, you need to be training future assistant directors and directors, and if you are a teacher, you need to be training assistant teachers and substitutes to become full-time teachers.

If you are holding your team members back, you are hurting your center.

A leader is never afraid of someone outshining them because when the team shines, the light is always reflected back to the leader. We have seen first-hand directors that are threatened by team members with strong leadership qualities; they feel that this person could do a better job than them.

If you are holding your team members back, you are hurting your center. Everyone brings certain strengths and weaknesses to the center, and a good leader will identify a team member's strengths and weaknesses and make sure that the right person is always doing the right job at the right time.

If a team member has incredible people skills and the director does not, that team member should be doing the tours. The director should never feel threatened by this, she should be empowered by the fact that she has the right person in the right seat for the betterment of the organization. **T.E.A.M.** is an acronym for **Together Everyone Achieves More**. In a team, there are no individuals and you all work together for the common good.

Always be looking for opportunities to train staff members for future leadership positions. If you are a teacher, ask your director what opportunities you have for future advancement at your school and see what financial help may be available. You may already be director qualified but are scared to step into that role because you have never had leadership training. We would recommend reading as many Dr. John C. Maxwell books on leadership as you can, that will help you to develop amazing leadership qualities.

Remember this important gem on leadership: **Continually train future leaders.**

Gem #78

Invest in Leadership Training

"An investment in knowledge pays the best interest."

~ Benjamin Franklin

Leading others may come naturally to some people, but for most, it has to be learned. Most child care leaders have never had one minute of leadership training in their life and wonder why they are having problems leading others. Leadership takes time to master and you can never get too much training in this area.

> *Leadership takes time to master and you can never get too much training in this area.*

There are several books we are going to recommend to you to help develop your leadership skills. If you are an owner, you will become better at working with your leadership team. If you are a director, you will become more effective at leading your team. If you are a teacher, you will become better at managing your classroom. You will also become a better follower by becoming a better leader.

The first book we recommend is *The 15 Invaluable Laws of Growth* by Dr. John C. Maxwell. Personal growth is paramount to effective leadership and that is the perfect place to start.

The next book you would want to read is *The 21 Irrefutable Laws of Leadership* by Dr. John C. Maxwell. This book is the top leadership book in the world and will give you the skills to lead a team of hundreds of people someday.

Leadership is about influence and sometimes you have

to influence those above you, and that is where Dr. John C. Maxwell's book *The 360 Degree Leader* will help you.

Here are some other books by Dr. John C. Maxwell that are all great leadership books: *The 21 Indispensable Qualities of a Leader, Leadership 101, Developing the Leader Within You* and *Developing the Leaders Around You.*

Do you notice a pattern? Dr. John C. Maxwell books on growth, personal development and leadership are some of the best in the world. You can never go wrong reading one of his books, it will help you to become more valuable to your employer which in turn puts more money in your paycheck.

Remember this important gem on leadership: **Invest in leadership training.**

Gem #79

Empower Others to Succeed

"When leaders fail to empower others, it is usually due to three main reasons: 1. desire for job security 2. resistance to change 3. lack of self-worth."

~ John C. Maxwell

A rising tide lifts all boats; the more you empower your team with leadership, the more it helps everyone on the team. To become a director in our industry you must have a desire to empower others to succeed.

If you are an owner or director, there is the type of person you want to avoid in giving a leadership role. You must avoid a person that has little self-worth. You want someone with confidence. Otherwise, that person will not want to empower others for fear of being replaced.

Someone with little self-worth will also be resistant to

change. Any organization in our industry who refuses to change will quickly go out of business.

> *To become a director in our industry you must have a desire to empower others to succeed.*

There are tests you can give potential leaders to see what natural strengths they possess. People skills and strategic thinking are two of the most important ones. You need a director or assistant director that can relate to parents on a tour and also help you with marketing and advertising.

Purchase the book *Strengthsfinder 2.0* and in the book, there will be a coupon code to take an assessment test online. Give a copy of the book to all of your leaders and potential leaders. Knowing who has what strengths will be paramount to making sure that you are empowering the right people in leadership positions.

If you are a teacher or assistant teacher and you want to someday become a director or assistant director, tell your owner! Find out what you need to do to one day have a leadership role in your company. State your case clearly why would want to be considered, making sure to talk about how it would benefit them. Get yourself the necessary credentials and read every leadership book you can get your hands on. Remember the saying *"If it's to be it's up to me."* No one is going to give you anything in this world, you are going to have to work for it. Work hard on empowering others on your team and you are well on your way to someday leading your own amazing team.

Remember this important gem on leadership: **Empower others to succeed.**

Gem #80

Empathy & Compassion are Important Leadership Qualities

"If you want to be the best leader you can possibly be, no matter how much or how little natural leadership talent you possess, you need to become a serving leader."

~ John C. Maxwell

Empathy and compassion are two skills that set apart an amazing director from an average director in our industry. Those with these amazing gifts, in our opinion, make the absolute best leaders in early childhood education.

Empathy is the ability to understand and share the feelings of another person. A leader needs to feel pain, pleasure, happiness, and sadness from another person and be able to comfort them or cheer with them when needed.

> *Serving others is the best way to develop empathy and compassion.*

Compassion is a concern for the suffering and misfortune of others. When a child gets hurt at school and you have to call the parents and tell them, compassion needs to kick in so you can *"feel their pain."* When a teacher tells you her husband has cancer you need to have compassion and *"feel her pain."*

If you can cry when hearing about the pain of someone else or you can have joy in your heart when others succeed, you have the right qualities to be a leader in our industry.

If you have a cold heart and do not have any emotional feelings towards others, there is nothing wrong with you, that is the way you are wired. You may be an amazing teacher but more than likely you will struggle at leading a team because it is hard to respect someone you cannot have an emotional connection with.

Serving others is the best way to develop empathy and compassion. Work hard to always try to bring value to others in all communication. Remember many of the gems in this book as they were written to help you live your best life and make you better at your job.

Remember this important gem on leadership: **Empathy and compassion are important leadership qualities.**

Gem #81

Have a Leader's Attitude

"The leader's attitude is like a thermostat for the place she works. If her attitude is good, the atmosphere is pleasant, and the environment is easy to work in. But if her attitude is bad, the temperature is insufferable."

~ John C. Maxwell

If you are in a leadership position at your company, you are not allowed to have a bad day. Your attitude dictates the attitude of every single person that works for you. If you are a teacher the same goes for you. When you are having a bad day, the kids sense it and will step on your very last nerve.

Attitude is a state of mind and you are the one that controls your thoughts. Do not allow negative thoughts to creep into your mind at work, ever. Place positive sayings on that walls around your workspace. Read them many times a day, out loud, so that your brain hears them clearly. Your mind cannot have a positive and a negative thought at the same exact time. So whenever a negative thought creeps in, drown it out with a positive thought and you will immediately feel better.

If you are an owner or in a leadership position, your team needs to always see you with a positive attitude. Your attitude is the thermometer of the workplace. If the leader is in a great mood, the team is happy. If the leader is in a bad mood, everyone is miserable.

> *If you are an owner or in a leadership position, your team needs to always see you with a positive attitude.*

It is not fair to place the burden of your negative attitude onto those you work with. Start reading positive books, work on improving your self-image, and practice some of the things in this book on your mindset like positive self-talk. Dr. John Maxwell has several books on attitude, an excellent one is *The Difference Maker: Making Your Attitude Your Greatest Asset.*

Remember this important gem on leadership: **Have a leader's attitude.**

Gem #82

Dealing With Parents Can be Tricky

"Good leaders know when to display emotions and when to delay them."

~ *John C. Maxwell*

You are 82% of the way done with this book, congratulations. I hope you are seeing a change in the way you are starting to look at yourself and your surroundings.

Unfortunately, the parents you have to deal with more than likely will not have read this book, and more than likely have never read any positive mental attitude books.

As you start to apply the gems in this book into your life you will start to notice the people around you may start to seem overly negative. The truth is they have always been like that, but you used to be that way as well and never noticed.

> *The more of a positive person you become, the more you will not be able to stand to be around negative people.*

Keep in mind that, when a parent lashes out at you, they are not doing it to you personally, they are hurting in some area of their life and you are just collateral damage. Maybe their boss yelled at them this morning, maybe her husband wants a divorce, maybe a family member has a health issue. A lot of times when a parent is yelling at a staff member, the issue they are mad about is not the real issue, so you must not display emotion and you have to keep your attitude under control. The natural reaction will be to fight back when attacked, but losing your cool is a disaster that you do not want to happen. The next day things will be calmed down, so be sure to ask if they are okay and you are concerned. Doing so will oftentimes trigger an apology and everything will go back to normal.

One area you will struggle with is a negative parent. The more of a positive person you become, the more you will not be able to stand to be around negative people. Unfortunately, you will have to deal with the parents of the children you are teaching, so you will have to learn the art of deflection. When the conversation turns negative, deflect the conversation in a more positive direction by talking about something amazing their child did that day. It is hard for a parent to complain when their child is being praised.

The more positive you are the more chance it has to rub off on others. When a parent asks you why you are always in a good mood, recommend John C. Maxwell's book *The 15 Invaluable Laws of Growth* and tell them it will change their life. Whatever you do, do not let them bring you down to their level; bring them up to yours!

Remember this important gem on leadership: **Dealing with parents can be tricky.**

Teresa & Jillian's Story

Because she was one of the most seasoned early educators at Leapfrog, Teresa was a role model of excellence when it came to parent communication and relationships. Jillian felt very lucky to be Teresa's teacher-team partner, because it enabled her to model the skillful language and behaviors Teresa used to win parents over. Plus, Teresa was a master of building rapport and trust during the phone call and the tour with visiting new parents.

Teresa worked with Donna to create a teacher training on Parent Communication that they presented at the next staff meeting. One fantastic technique was known as L-A-S-T which is based on the actual system that Disney uses to resolve customer complaints. (Donna knew this because she had attended a leadership seminar at Disney in Orlando and brought the method back to her team.) L-A-S-T stands for Listen, Apologize, Solve, and Thank.

Teresa was a master of L-A-S-T. Any time she sensed a parent was even mildly upset or disappointed, she went into problem-solving mode. She used empathy to get parents to open up and she actively listened to the words they used. She apologized, even if she felt like she did nothing wrong. Teresa and Jillian worked together when they could to creatively solve parent issues and complaints. Donna was SO appreciative of their efforts to take this off her shoulders even a little bit. Jillian was learning the techniques, and the team had a great retention rate of children and families.

Gem #83

Harness the Power of Persuasion

"When people respect you as a person, they admire you. When they respect you as a friend, they love you. When they respect you as a leader, they follow you."

~ *John C. Maxwell*

One of the hardest things to do in leadership is to get someone to do something you want them to do when they do not want to do it. The secret to persuading others to your way of thinking is through getting them to respect you as a leader.

> *One of the hardest things to do in leadership is to get someone to do something you want them to do when they do not want to do it.*

In this chapter, we learned a lot about leadership and how it is different from being a boss. Leaders are respected, bosses are normally feared. If you are instilling fear into your team members you have no respect and may never be able to lead them effectively without a lot of hard work.

John C. Maxwell wrote an amazing book called *How to Influence People*. It is an amazing resource for you to learn how to use the power of persuasion to get your team members to do things even when they do not want to.

You will notice a common theme in this book, we refer a lot to Dr. John C. Maxwell's books. The reason is simple, he is the best author in the world on leadership and mindset. When you are finished with this book you have not arrived, far from it.

You have taken the first step, but there are a lot more steps to get you where you need to go. Once this book is a distant memory, our wish for you is that you become a student of some of Dr. John C. Maxwell's books and let them help you to go places in life and lead others.

Remember this important gem on leadership: **Harness the power of persuasion.**

Gem #84

Don't Micromanage Staff

"If you can't influence people, then they will not follow you. And if people won't follow, you are not a leader. That's the Law of Influence."

~ *John C. Maxwell*

One of the most sure-fire ways to lose the respect of your subordinates is to micro-manage them. This tells them you do not trust them to do the job without you checking on them.

We like to use the saying, trust but verify. When we assign a teacher a task to do, we tell her that we are going to be checking on her progress at certain intervals and would like an update at that time. By telling her you are going to be checking in with her it lets her know you are not micromanaging but are seeing if there is any help or guidance you can offer.

If you are an owner and you trust your director, leave them alone and let them lead.

Communication is very important when tasks are assigned. The project should be in writing with clear expectations for the scope of the project, who to report to, how often to report in, and what the finished product should look like, and what the deadline for completion is. Let there be no gray area that could cause confusion because that is bad for everyone.

Always be sure to let the person you are assigning a project to know that you are available anytime she has a question and that you are confident the project will be done on time to complete satisfaction.

The most micromanaging we have seen in our years as Child Care Coaches is from owners to directors. If you are an owner and you trust your director, leave them alone and let them lead. Micromanaging means a lack of trust and when you do not trust your director, you have lost their respect. Look back at some of the gems we have written here and let go of the vine and trust your team, they have your back.

Remember this important gem on leadership: **Don't micromanage staff.**

Gem #85

Be Humble

"The best leaders are humble enough to realize their victories depend upon their people."

~ *John C. Maxwell*

A leader is a humble servant of all of his or her team members. A true leader reflects recognition down to the team members in his or her organization. A true leader never boasts about herself or her accomplishments, it is all about the team. Being humble is a sure fire way to garnish respect of your team.

As a leader, you will never succeed at anything without your team members. If you gain accreditation, they deserve the credit. Have a flawless inspection? The team gets the credit. Get another quality rating star? The team should be recognized. There is power in recognizing the team in all center accomplishments, owners and directors should never take any of the credit.

To be an effective leader, be humble and be like a mirror. When someone recognizes you, thank them and immediately hold up a mirror to reflect the recognition to everyone on the team because nothing is possible without everyone working together.

As a leader, you will never succeed at anything without your team members.

Remember this important gem on leadership: **Be humble.**

Chapter 5 Notes:

_____

_____

_____

_____

_____

_____

_____

_____

_____

_____

_____

_____

_____

_____

_____

_____

_____

Chapter 6

Work Ethic

"Developing a good work ethic is key to success. Apply yourself at whatever you do, whether you're a janitor or taking your first summer job because that work ethic will be reflected in everything you do in life."

~ *Tyler Perry*

work eth·ic · *noun*

1. The principle that hard work is intrinsically virtuous or worthy of reward.

Ask 10 teachers what work ethic is and you will more than likely get 10 different responses. Not only do definitions differ, but expectations of what work ethic actually is would also vary from person to person as well.

As owners, we want employees who are honest, trustworthy, hardworking, compassionate, and caring. As teachers, we would like co-workers to pull their own weight, show up on time, have a great attitude, and love on the children daily.

We have both noticed over the last 10-15 years, a shift in

the work ethic of today's younger staff members. It seems that more and more of them have poor work performance, cannot get to work on time, lie or cheat, and have no respect for others.

If you are reading this, please do not be someone who lacks an incredible work ethic. If you are a director, you should be setting the example of what a near perfect work ethic should look like. If you are an owner be sure to ask questions related to work ethic in the job interview and hire based on this attribute.

In this chapter, you will learn some tips on how you can have an incredible work ethic. If you take the gems on mindset we have given you, couple them with the leadership gems and then incorporate these work ethic gems into everything you do, the sky's the limit. You will get higher pay, more responsibility, and a lot more recognition.

Gem #86

Never Lie, Cheat or Steal

"Here are the values that I stand for: honesty, equality, kindness, compassion, treating people the way you want to be treated and helping those in need. To me, those are traditional values."

~ *Ellen DeGeneres*

If you are a teacher, be sure that you properly sign in and sign out for the day.

As an owner, having an employee steal from you is the worst feeling in the world. This is someone that you have trusted, and they have betrayed you and everyone else that works for the company.

In life, there is a golden rule

that will help you to succeed, and that rule states you should never under any circumstances lie, cheat, or steal. If you are an owner this goes for you as well, never lie to your employees or try to cheat them on payroll by stealing hours they have worked.

If you are a teacher, be sure that you properly sign in and sign out for the day. Nothing bothers an owner more than employees sitting around at the end of the day trying to pad their paychecks with a few extra minutes. That is stealing from your employer!

"The measure of a man's real character is what he would do if he knew he would never be found out."

~ Thomas B Macaulay

Some other examples of lying, cheating or stealing from your employer: making copies for personal use, using company time to do personal errands, making long distance calls on company phones, eating food that is made for the children, padding your timecard to give yourself extra hours not actually worked, taking tuition money that does not belong to you, and taking supplies home or using them for personal use without permission.

Remember this important gem on work ethic: **Never lie, cheat or steal.**

Gem #87

Give Your Team Your Best You

"Professionalism shouldn't be defined by a person's paycheck, role or title. It should be defined by a person's work ethic."

~ Janna Cachola

If you expect to receive 100% of your paycheck each payday then be sure to give 100% to your employer each and every day.

Children are normally happy by nature because society has not beaten them down yet. Take a lesson from the children, be happy and enjoy each day. Each day children just want to have fun, and as a teacher, director, cook, aide, or an owner, you need to have the same goal, have fun each day and love what you do.

"I believe that when you do what you love, you find higher levels of satisfaction that can compensate for lower income."

~Adam Neumann

> *Your team is counting on you to be your best version of you each and every day.*

It is much more important to love a job working for less money than to hate a job that pays you a lot more. There is incredible value in working at a job you love.

Your team is counting on you to be your best version of you each and every day. Remember, a chain is only as strong as its weakest link. Do not be the weak link in your center, give your best and encourage others to do the same. Doing so will yield incredible results.

Remember this important gem on work ethic: **Give your team your best you.**

Gem #88

Calling out Sick Means Actually Being Sick

"It's just the way we are, the way we were raised. Our work ethic was everything, and that never left us. We like to work hard, and we like to try to do everything 100 percent."

~Mary-Kate and Ashley Olsen

Employee call outs are the single most stressful part of running a child care center. In most businesses, when an employee calls out it is not such a big deal, someone else can normally pick up the slack. At a child care center minimum staff to child ratios make it very hard to adequately staff when employees call out sick, especially when there are multiple callouts in a single day.

If you have a high fever and are throwing up, we are okay with you staying home, providing you can give at least two hours notice to your director or owner prior to your shift. If you are an opener, you may have to come to work and ask to go home early. It is a lot harder to cover an opener in that short of time.

> *Do not leave your team members to pick up your slack!*

If you need to call in sick do not text or leave a voicemail, it may not be received. We encourage all centers to have a policy that you have to talk to a live person (a minimum of two hours prior to the start of shift) to call out sick. This way you are 100% certain that the message is received and there is time to get a replacement in.

Never call in *"slick."* Calling in slick means you tell your employer you are sick when you actually want to go to the beach or do something fun. NEVER DO THIS! Do it the proper way and request time off. Honesty is always the best policy when it comes to time off. Do not leave your team members to pick up your slack!

If you are a director or owner please immediately terminate anyone who you catch calling in sick that is not actually sick. There is nothing more deceitful than someone who makes co-workers pick up extra slack without going through proper time off procedures.

Remember this important gem on work ethic: **Calling in sick means actually being sick.**

Gem #89

Don't be a Stereotypical Millennial

"Above all, we want Millennials to realize that they can have an impact on the world and that, in the course of empowering others, they can also empower themselves."

~ Nicholas Kristof

Anyone born between 1981 and 1996 is considered a millennial, and you have gotten a bad rap over the years. One of the biggest complaints we have received from owners is that millennials have incredibly poor work ethics.

> *If you have a great work ethic as a cornerstone, you can become anything you want to in life.*

We have written this book specifically to help you change your mindset and become your best you. If you take the gems we have written to heart and practice them daily, no one will ever be able to label you as a typical millennial. You will have a great work ethic. You will work harder than everyone else. You will have incredible confidence and a huge degree of self-worth. You are amazing and the world will know it.

If you have a great work ethic as a cornerstone, you can become anything you want to in life. It takes so very little to be above average today, just having a strong work ethic will make you stand out head and shoulders above the crowd.

Make a commitment today to be a better version of yourself going forward; one with a positive mindset and an incredible work ethic. Forget what society has labeled you as, prove them wrong. Set your future goals and go for them. You can do anything in life you want to do, but it starts with a dream, a goal, and then a plan of action. Lastly, work like crazy until you succeed.

Remember this important gem on work ethic: **Don't be a stereotypical millennial.**

Gem #90

Protect Your Social Media

"Social media is changing the way we communicate and the way we are perceived, both positively and negatively. Every time you post a photo or update your status, you are contributing to your own digital footprint and personal brand."

~ Amy Jo Martin

We both grew up in a simpler time. Our children cannot understand how we grew up without a cell phone, microwaves, computers, a flat-screen TV, social media, and 250 channels.

You don't know what you don't know, so we played the hand we were dealt. There will be technology in 20 years that you would not believe if someone told you today, just like if someone told us when we were teenagers that we would have 70" flat screen televisions and we would carry phones in our pockets that store 256 billion bits of information. We would have told you were crazy.

> *With every post, you are painting a picture of yourself to the world.*

Social media has been good and bad in terms of contribution to society. Personally, we think it has done more harm than good. The funny thing about social media is that we normally only show the world our best self, sometimes fabricating things to make ourselves look better, yet we think everyone else is always telling the truth.

With every post, you are painting a picture of yourself to the world. Do not believe privacy settings, nothing is private on the internet. What picture do you want the world to see of you?

Never post anything you would not want your mother, grandmother, neighbors, current or future employers, future boyfriends or girlfriends to read. We have seen countless times in our lives a social media post someone made in their 20s that seemed harmless come back to bite them later in life.

As an employer, you should never hire anyone without checking social media first. You are looking for a pattern of questionable behavior. If someone would show the world questionable behavior, what would they show to your customers?

We know a child care center owner who found out on social media that two of his employees were strippers in the evening. Imagine the uproar if parents found out that their child's teacher was a stripper. Your initial thought might be that you should be allowed to do whatever you want in your off time, and you would be correct. You can do whatever you want to do in your off time. If you want to work for me as a teacher, there is a certain standard of acceptable behavior that we expect you to represent on and off the clock.

Whenever you comment on someone else's post, that too becomes a matter of public record for eternity. A good rule of thumb is to only post or comment on things of a positive nature and never post or comment on anything you would not read on the 6:00 news for the world to see.

The internet is full of creeps, stalkers, rapists, murderers, and bad people. Using check-ins tells the world where you are at a given time which is never a good idea. Posting where you will be and when you will be there also tells the world that you will not be home at a certain time and that is bad as well. If you are going to post pics from a concert you go to, it is much better to wait until you get home to post them than to do it and tell the world you are not home at the moment.

If you're in your twenties, please note that you are extra susceptible to the influences of friends in terms of social media behavior and norms. We want you to make great choices for the long term success of your professional life. What may seem harmless to you now could have devastating effects later in life. It is a dangerous world out there, please practice safe internet usage.

Remember this important gem on work ethic: **Protect your social media.**

Teresa & Jillian's Story

Jillian was a huge social media user, and she particularly loved SnapChat. After reading this gem, she asked her older sister for advice on social media behavior. After all, most things shared on SnapChat remain private – right? Jillian's sister Jenny told her that she herself had gotten mixed up in a bit of a social media controversy with a potential future employer. A couple years prior, she had posted some "*interesting*" pictures on Instagram that were meant to be artistic and funny. There was no nudity, but the pictures made Jenny seem to have poor judgement. The future employer saw the photos and decided not to hire Jenny based on what they saw.

Jillian decided to be more careful in the future with her posts, and asked her friends to do the same. After all, she was a role model to young children and she did not want any parents from the center seeing any questionable posts online. She loved her job at Leapfrog and didn't want to put it in jeopardy in any way.

Gem #91

Give Your Boss Proper Notice

"Even though your time on the job is temporary, if you do a good enough job, your work there will last forever."

~ *Idowu Koyenikan*

No one will work a job forever; as an owner, you should understand that eventually, everyone will leave you either through moving onto another job or by retiring.

> *It takes time to hire and train your replacement and the more experienced you are, the more time it will take.*

Whoever hired you thought enough of you to give you a job to put food on your table. This person invested time, energy and lots of money in training you.

An owner should never get upset with a staff member who chooses to leave employment, except if that person fails to give proper notice. It takes time to hire and train your replacement and the more experienced you are, the more time it will take. If you have been working at your center less than three years please give a minimum two-week notice to your employer when you wish to terminate employment.

If you are in a leadership position such as a director, assistant director or a lead or head teacher or have worked at your center more than 3 years, you need to give your employer a minimum of a four-week notice. Why would you need to give a four-week notice? Common courtesy because it will take a minimum of four weeks to hire and train your replacement properly.

We encourage owners and directors to make a deal with all of their employees and talk about it every time you have a staff training. If you leave the company and give proper notice, we will hire you back in the future if the new job does not work out. Failure to give a required notice means there is no way on God's green earth you are coming back to work for us and we will make sure when any future employer calls us looking for a reference we will tell that person that they are not eligible for rehire.

If you are an owner or director, we would recommend coming up with a similar policy in your company. Be sure when someone does give notice you do an exit interview and find out the real reason they are leaving. Make sure you let them know that they are welcome back anytime and that you appreciate everything they have done.

Never get upset with someone who gives notice. Getting upset with this person guarantees they would never want to come back. Always part on good terms and if they were a very good employee, give them a call after they are working at that job for three weeks to see how they are doing. If they are unhappy, it will manifest at the three-week mark. If they say they do not like the job, offer them their old job back for the same pay and benefits, you have nothing to lose.

Remember this important gem on work ethic: **Give your boss proper notice.**

Gem #92

Character is Everything

"Authenticity is everything! You have to wake up every day and look in the mirror, and you want to be proud of the person who's looking back at you. And you can only do that if you're being honest with yourself and being a person of high character. You have an opportunity every single day to write that story of your life."

~ Aaron Rodgers

An owner always wants all of the staff members to have the highest possible character at all times, on and off the clock. Never forget your mission, to educate the next generation to be better than we were at their age.

> *Having character is doing what is right, all of the time, even when you know no one is watching you.*

Many of the gems in this book, when lived in your daily life, will help to mold your character into one of the highest caliber. Be sure to always have the utmost honesty and integrity, show initiative and do more than what is asked of you.

Come to work with a smile on your face and with an amazing attitude. Having character is doing what is right, all of the time, even when you know no one is watching you.

You are charged with one of the most important jobs in human history: educating the next generation. Children will imitate what they see. Your own children will model your behavior. Teaching a child to have the utmost character in everything they do will help them to live a very rewarding life.

Remember this important gem on work ethic: **Character**

is everything.

Gem #93

Remember the Extra Degree

"At 211 degrees, water is hot. At 212 degrees, it boils. And with boiling water, comes steam... and with steam, you can power a train. One degree. Applying one extra degree of temperature to water means the difference between something that is simply very hot and something that generates enough force to power a machine."

~ Sam Parker, 212 The Extra Degree

Water heated to 212° Fahrenheit will boil. This is the law of physics and no matter what we do, we cannot change it. What happens if we heat water up to 211°? We have hot water.

Water heated to 211° is simply that, hot water. What happens if you continue heating the 211-degree water up one more degree? It boils. At 212° Fahrenheit boiling water creates steam, which will spin turbines that can produce electricity or turn a propeller shaft. Boiling water can light up a city and move ships and trains around the world.

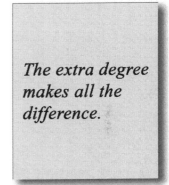

The extra degree makes all the difference.

The extra degree makes all the difference. Look for areas in your life where you can apply the extra degree philosophy. At work, you can show initiative and do more than is asked of you. Owners love it when staff members take initiative and give the extra degree of work performance.

When applying the extra degree principle, do not forget about your personal life. In your relationships, never settle for average. Find someone who uplifts you, values you and cherishes you. Find things you can do to bring value to others, such as volunteering your time for causes that you hold near and dear to your heart. The extra degree of effort makes all the difference.

Every time you boil water, think of this analogy and incorporate it into your daily life. Doing so will open doors for you that you could never have imagined. The world is an empty canvas; go forth and paint a picture of the rest of your life in whatever colors you choose.

We would highly recommend reading the book, *212° The Extra Degree* by Sam Parker; it will change your life.

Remember this important gem on work ethic: **Remember the extra degree.**

Gem #94

Inspections are Positive Experiences

"A positive attitude causes a chain reaction of positive thoughts, events, and outcomes. It is a catalyst and it sparks extraordinary results."

~ Wade Boggs

When a licensing inspector shows up, it is time to be on your absolute best behavior. Inspections are very important and have a specific purpose: to ensure that children are cared for in a safe environment. Having a positive attitude is a good way for the inspector to be pleasant back to you.

When an inspector shows up it is time to make sure that your classroom is picked up and in compliance with all licensing rules. As a teacher, this is your responsibility. If the inspector speaks to you be friendly but never stop your primary responsibility of watching the children. Never take your eyes off of the children while speaking to a licensing inspector.

Never volunteer any information. Be friendly and never combative. Sometimes the inspector will "*go fishing*" and ask you questions to see if you or your center have been breaking the rules. Only answer what is asked of you and nothing more.

> *Never take your eyes off of the children while speaking to a licensing inspector.*

If you are a director/owner it is important for you to follow the inspector around (insist on it) and know everything that is said. Any violations need to be addressed and fixed immediately to ensure you stay on an inspector's good side.

Remember this important gem on work ethic: **Inspections are positive experiences.**

Gem #95

Live Your Company's Core Values

"Education without values, as useful as it is, seems rather to make man a more clever devil."

~ C. S. Lewis

Core values are important for a child care center to have. We encourage all of our coaching clients to create 5-7 core values which your center stands for. These values need to be posted for the world to see and every employee should know them by heart and practice them each and every day.

If your center does not have core values, we encourage you to speak with your owner/director and encourage them to create them. Core values are something that everyone in the company should have a hand in creating because staff members are the ones that have to live up to them. The more involved the staff is at creating them, the more buy-in they will have. A good book to recommend to your owner/director to read to learn more about how to create core values is called *Built on Values,* by Ann Rhoades.

> *Core values are important for a child care center to have.*

If your center does have them, be sure you have them memorized and practice them in your daily life, both in and out of the classroom. Be sure that the parents of the children whom you teach know what your core values are because that is the standard of excellence they should expect each and every day.

Creating core values in a company will increase staff retention, especially if you hire, fire, reward, discipline and evaluate staff solely based on core values. It is a game changer for your business, we can promise you.

Remember this important gem on work ethic: **Live your company's core values.**

Gem #96

It is Not a Competition

"I'm not in a competition with anybody but myself. My goal is to beat my last performance."

~ Celine Dion

No one benefits from unhealthy competition. We both have seen this with clients that we coach. We have also seen it between owners of different schools.

If you work for a single location center every teacher is on the same team. There should never be any competition between teachers and never any jealousy over anything. We have seen many times one teacher mad because another teacher got better supplies or a better schedule.

Remember that at the end of the day everyone is on the same team.

If you work for a center with multiple locations, we have seen the same level of competition between locations. We have seen teachers who are unfriendly to substitutes from another center because they consider them outsiders. We recommend centers with multiple locations have a policy that everyone works for the company, not for a location.

Remember that at the end of the day everyone is on the same team. Never be jealous of anyone for any reason at all. An owner or director makes decisions based on many factors, which are rarely discussed with team members when changes are made. If you are asked to make a change, do so with a positive attitude. Trust your owner/director to make these kinds of decisions without any drama. Never be jealous of anyone you perceive to have it better than you; it is not a competition.

Remember this important gem on work ethic: **It is not a competition.**

Teresa & Jillian's Story

As part of their ongoing professional development journey, Teresa and Jillian read the book *Move Your Bus* by world-renowned teacher Ron Clark. They learned about the concept of runners, joggers, walkers, and riders. Both women shared their desire to be "*runners*" at Leapfrog. They had a deep admiration and love for their director, Donna, as well as all the children and families they cared for. They agreed that they could both thrive and do well in their careers at Leapfrog without feeling like they needed to compete with one another. They approached work and life with a "*rising tide lifts all boats*" philosophy.

A few months after finishing this book, Teresa got promoted to Assistant Director to help Donna in the administrative management and leadership of the school. She specialized in enrollment and parent relationships, and she received consistent bonuses for each enrollment she secured, which added up to a nice nest egg. Jillian was very happy for her. Jillian got promoted to Lead Teacher of the Pre-K classroom and she was one of the youngest Lead Teachers of any program in the area.

Both women had made huge leaps forward in their personal and professional accomplishments. They were proud of themselves, had money in the bank, were on a health and fitness journey, had great relationships with their loved ones, and started mentoring other teachers who wanted to model their success. When they were having a tough day, they sought each other out for a hug, and re-read the various gems in this book to keep feeding their positive mindsets.

Gem #97

Get your Financial House in Order

"A budget tells us what we can't afford, but it doesn't keep us from buying it."

~ William Feather

In all of our years in the child care business, we have noticed a pattern with a lot of teachers, many of them were incredibly bad with money. Financial mismanagement, especially at an early age, will create life long problems if not managed properly.

We weren't quite sure which chapter to put this gem in so we decided that work ethic was the best suited. When your finances are a mess you normally are stressed and your work will suffer because of it.

We want to give you some advice that will help you become better at money management and create a lot less stress in your life. Follow a few simple strategies from this point forward, no matter how old you are or how close you are to retiring.

> *The younger you are, the more financial advantages you will have available to you.*

The younger you are, the more financial advantages you will have available to you. How is that possible? Time. Someone under 25 has the power of time on their side much more than someone over 40. When money earns interest it grows, but when the interest starts earning interest, well, that is when wealth is created.

The average person in America with a high school diploma will earn one million dollars in a lifetime. Someone with a

Bachelor's Degree will earn around two million dollars in a lifetime and someone with a Master's Degree can earn over three million dollars in a lifetime.

If you do not have a degree, consider getting one. Even if a Bachelor's Degree were to cost you $100k you would still be $900k to the positive in your lifetime. Do not look at the cost of school as an expense; it is an investment that pays dividends.

You do not have to quit your job to go to college; many people do it online while having a full-time job.

The next thing you need to learn is delayed gratification. If you cannot pay for it today, you cannot afford it. Stop financing things over time. You cannot afford a $1,000 phone when you only make $10 an hour. You cannot afford a new car if you only make $10 an hour.

There is nothing wrong with owning an older phone and driving an older car. We know what you're thinking: what will my friends think of me? Who cares, they do not pay your bills, do they?

If you want a new car; save for it. If you want a new phone; pay cash for it and do not pay for it monthly. Consider using layaway to get Christmas gifts, you can pay on it each week until it is paid off. That is delayed gratification.

Never use a credit card unless you intend to pay 100% of the balance off each month. Paying credit card interest is not financially smart. Credit card companies are loan sharks, loaning you money at ridiculous interest rates. If you are carrying balances, make a commitment today to cut up the card and pay off the balance as fast as you can.

Paying taxes is not fun, yet we have to do it. Paying the least amount of taxes is a smart financial decision. The IRS has a great way for you to pay fewer taxes and create wealth in the process; it is called retirement savings. If your employer offers a retirement plan, please contribute the maximum allowable by law each and every year. Often times the employer will match some of the contributions, which is free money!

If your employer does not have a retirement plan, create your own. Open an individual IRA account and contribute the maximum each year, which is fully tax-deferred until you take the money out, which you cannot do under any circumstances until you are retirement age or there will be financial penalties.

Have a savings account as well and contribute to it each payday. Start with as little as $10 a week and every time you get a raise for the rest of your life take half of your raise and invest or save it and take the other half and increase your lifestyle. If you do this your whole life you will be a wealthy person at retirement. Ask your bank to set up an auto transfer to savings each payday so it is done without you having to think about it.

Everyone needs to have a budget. Write out all of your expenses (including retirement and savings) on a sheet of paper. Next, figure out what your monthly income is. Now figure out if you have enough to cover all of your bills, if not, you may have to work some overtime or get a second job.

If you follow these things we have laid out for you, finances will Rarely become a problem for you. You may have to buy second-hand clothes or use a second-hand cell phone, but you will be much better off financially in a few years than someone who overspends and becomes indebted to credit card companies.

Remember this important gem on finances: **Get your financial house in order.**

Chapter 6 Notes:

Chapter 7

Resources for Continued Growth

"I would never read a book if it were possible for me to talk a half an hour with the man that wrote it."

~ *Woodrow Wilson*

Gem #98

For Owners Only

If you are a child care center owner, we want to thank you for purchasing this book and we would like to encourage you to buy a copy of this book for every staff member at your center. Make this book required reading as part of your onboarding process and watch your retention rate increase. Please write a personal note on page iii to your team member letting them know what a valuable staff member they are. This book will change their lives and they will be indebted to you for giving it to them!

We would like to encourage you to read Brian Duprey's first book *Child Care Millionaire* and either of Kris Murray's books *The 77 Best Strategies to Grow your Early Childhood Program, The Ultimate Child Care Marketing Guide, and Rock Star Stories.*

We would also encourage you to read our friend Sindye Alexander's book called *Relationship Roadmap: Real-World Strategies for Building a Positive, Collaborative Culture in Your Preschool.* This is the best book in our industry for helping you with staff culture and retention. We would encourage you to purchase a copy for all of the members of your leadership team.

The next resource we have available is a free podcast. Kris Murray's Child Care Rockstar Radio™ is the top child care podcast on the internet and is a free resource for you. Visit Google Play or the App Store.

If you own a center licensed for more than 49 children, we would like to offer you a complimentary Strategy Session Coaching Call. One of our trained coaches will take 30-45 minutes and walk you through some strategies to help you get over some of the things that are causing you pain or frustration in your business. You will leave the call with actionable plans you can put in place right away in your business. This session is 100% complimentary and is our gift to you. You can register by visiting www.childcaresuccess.com.

We also want to encourage you to attend Kris Murray's Child Care Success Summit, which is held in the fall each year. This is the world's largest conference 100% devoted to the business side of child care. You can get more information and purchase tickets at www.childcaresuccesssummit.com. We both speak at this conference annually as well as dozens of top speakers in our industry. We are looking forward to meeting you there so please come up and introduce yourself.

Gem #99

Recommended Reading

"Books are the quietest and most constant of friends; they are the most accessible and wisest of counselors, and the most patient of teachers."

~ *Charles W. Eliot*

Amazing Child Care Books:
- *The Ultimate Child Care Marketing Guide – Kris Murray*
- *Child Care Millionaire - Brian Duprey*
- *The 77 Best Strategies to Grow your Early Childhood Program – Kris Murray*
- *Relationship Roadmap: Real World Strategies for Cultivating a Positive and Collaborative Culture in Your Preschool - Sindye Alexander*
- *Rock Star Stories - Kris Murray*

Leadership & Mindset Books by Dr. John C. Maxwell:
- *Developing the Leaders Around You*
- *Developing the Leader Within You*
- *Put Your Dream to the Test*
- *Sometimes You Win, Sometimes You Learn*
- *The 21 Irrefutable Laws of Leadership*
- *The 15 Invaluable Laws of Growth*
- *Today Matters*
- *Intentional Living*
- *The 360 Degree Leader*

- *The 17 Essential Qualities of a Team Player*
- *The 21 Indispensable Qualities of a Leader*
- *Becoming a Person of Influence*
- *Failing Forward*

Motivational Books by other authors we like:
- *The Slight Edge – Jeff Olson*
- *The Bible - God*
- *Leaders Eat Last – Simon Sinek*
- *Start with Why - Simon Sinek*
- *Awaken the Giant Within – Anthony Robbins*
- *The Power of Positive Thinking – Norman Vincent Peale*

Jake Chamberlain

Owner

Brighton Montessori

Brighton, MI

How long have you been in the child care Industry?

3 Years

Why do you love working in our industry?

I love the fact that many people in this industry are truly driven by making a difference in the lives of others. I also operate a business in a service industry that is more driven by the paycheck. I enjoy being able to be part of a group of people who are receptive to positive leadership and really appreciative of the opportunity to work in an organization that values its staff.

How do you keep a positive mindset at work?

Self-correction. I have to actively keep myself on course. It takes commitment and work. When I feel myself going into a negative space, I literally tell myself "I don't need to feel this way, I can be happy and move forward," and I magically am able to do just that.

What is your favorite PMA (Positive Mental Attitude) book?

The Slight Edge, by Jeff Olson.

When you are stressed at work, how do you de-stress?

Gratitude. You cannot be stressed and grateful at the same time. 99% of the time, whatever feels like stress is very small in the big scheme of things. I picture one of my children smiling and with that image in my mind, there is nothing that I cannot handle.

Favorite Positive Quote:

"Every morning on my nightstand are two stacks of dominos lined up. On the top of one it says you're a loser and the other says you're a winner. If I hit the snooze button, I've hit the first domino of the loser stack and my day is gonna suck. With that mentality, do you think I'm ever going to hit snooze again? Absolutely not!"

~ Bedros Keuilian

I love this metaphor. Your day always ends up going exactly how you start it. Hit that right stack of dominos!

If you could go back in time, what would you do differently next time?

I would put my ideas into action immediately rather than waiting for "the time to be right."

**Jennifer Sturman
(Slavin), M.Ed.**

Vice President of
Operations

Magic Memories Child
Development Centers

Phoenixville, PA

How long have you been in the child care industry?
15 years

Favorite hobby?
Spending time with family

Why do you love working in our industry?
I love this industry because I love those cute little kids and especially the teachers who long to teach them. I truly feel early childhood teachers are very special.

How do you keep a positive mindset at work?
My faith steers my path. Controlling what I allow to affect my thoughts and actions is how I maintain being positive. I am also very aware that my reaction or response is a huge factor in what the outcome will be.

What is your favorite PMA (Positive Mental Attitude) book?
My favorite PMA book is Think and Grow Rich by Napoleon Hill. I love how he simply conveys that with desire, faith, and persistence you can be successful in anything!

When you are stressed at work, how do you de-stress?

I de-stress in a few ways: unplugging from electronics, emails, texts, etc.; taking my mind away from those outside distractions; prayer; spending time with family and friends; and exercise.

What do you do for fun when not working?

I LOVE dating my husband. I love being at the beach. I love being with family and seeing friends.

Who is the one person you admire the most? why?

I truly admire my father, Donald Slavin. He is the definition of how desire, faith, and persistence can lead to success. He started out as a teenager who loved cars in the cleanup department of a car dealership to the President of Operations. He persisted in growing with the company and has moved mountains within it. He didn't really like school and never went to college but is the smartest man I know. One of his best qualities is that he always listens. He doesn't give up...on anyone or anything. His faith is his driving force which is evident in all his relationships and work. I'm so proud of him and so proud to be his daughter. I pray to be the parent that he and my mom were to me to my children and husband.

How has a positive mindset helped you with your career?

Having a positive mindset is the secret ingredient that everyone in early childhood is looking for!!! It is the reason I can form trusting relationships with my team, it gives our families a sense of love and security they look for, and the reason our centers and company can grow. Everything becomes possible!!

How has a positive mindset helped you with life in general?

It has simplified my life. By focusing on staying positive and losing the negative in life, I don't have the weight of stress and problems. Things become more clear. A problem has a solution. Things might not always be how I want them to be or have my ideal end result but leading with a positive mindset allows me to focus on what matters, not just what I want. No matter what, in the end, life is beautiful.

Jillian Lemos

Substitute Teacher

Little Angels Early
Learning Center

Bangor, ME

How long have you been in the child care industry?

I have been working officially in the childcare industry since March of 2017, when I first began employment with Little Angels. However, I have spent much of my life interacting with children, whether it be babysitting, volunteering at my Church's Bible Camp over the summer, or coaching youth soccer with my dad.

How do you keep a positive mindset at work?

For me, keeping a positive mindset at work is sort of like a snowball effect. I am typically a rather cheery and enthusiastic person to begin with, but once I hear someone say "I don't know how she has so much energy!" or compliments my attitude in some other way, it grows. Someone noting my good attitude turns it into a great attitude- especially if I feel as though someone else is benefitting from my cheeriness. When my goofiness, spontaneity, and energy lift others up, those characteristics grow.

What advice would you give to someone just starting out in the childcare industry?

Some advice that I would give someone just starting out in the childcare industry would be: HAVE FUN! You chose this job because you love kids, so let loose and let yourself enjoy the kids! These children will love you. The daycare will be a home away from home for them. When they ask to be picked up, pick them up. When they want a hug, hug them! If there is a child who is visibly upset- screaming and crying- get down on their level! Chances are, there is a problem that they will be able to articulate with a little bit of prompting. Ignoring the needs of a distressed child only adds to the problem. Children are people too. Communicate with them, ask what's wrong, and problem solve with them TOGETHER.

Favorite Positive Quote:

"I've got sunshine in my soul today" ~ Rosie Luik

How has a positive mindset helped you with life in general?

A positive mindset is helpful to me outside of work because it offers me the opportunity to help others. I find myself searching for the good in a situation more often than usual if I can sense that a friend or a peer is feeling down. I take great pride in people listening to my advice, and I love watching weight roll off someone's shoulders if I am able to help them work through a situation.

I love the quote "If you can't find the sunshine, be the sunshine" because I really feel as though helping others to find the sunshine is a huge source of joy in my life.

Joe Lawrence

Owner (former teacher)

Little Sprouts Academy

Menomonie, WI

How long have you been in the child care industry?
8 years

Why do you love working in our industry?
Our purpose statement is "Building people up so they may in turn build up others"... this industry is a great way to do that! That, and my days are never the same, there is always something exciting going on!

How do you keep a positive mindset at work?
By choice! Not getting caught up in emotions, calmly remembering past experiences and analyzing the situation to figure out where the hope is... it's always there if you choose to find it!

What is your favorite PMA (Positive Mental Attitude) book?
The Bible, there are so many good books out there... but there is so much wisdom in the Bible all throughout. From having hope, not fearing, not worrying, and EVEN to take heart in the midst of trials... "Count it all joy, my brothers, when you meet trials of various kinds, for you know that the testing of your faith produces steadfastness. And let steadfastness have its full effect, that you may be perfect and complete, lacking in nothing." - James 1:2-4

When you are stressed at work, how do you de-stress?

Work on something else. Take a break and clear my mind. I have a morning routine I like to do. Prayer, listening to/reading the Bible and positive leadership stuff, exercise, sitting in our little sauna.

Favorite Positive Quote:

"Have I not commanded you? Be strong and courageous. Do not be frightened, and do not be dismayed, for the Lord your God is with you wherever you go." Joshua 1:9

"Have a great day, or not... the choice is yours!"

If you could go back in time, what would you do differently next time?

To not worry so much, trust God more, and think about others even more!

What advice would you give for a new teacher on the importance of having a positive mindset?

It honestly is often the difference for many of either having an amazing time and getting paid for it or having a miserable time and burning out. Always look to have hope in situations, with team members, and for the children!

How has a positive mindset helped you with life in general?

Having hope in all things, which results in a positive mindset and confidence that God is looking out for me has made all the difference in the world. This makes for a more enjoyable life and hope for the future. I didn't say "easy", but more enjoyable embracing all things!

Marcia St.Hilaire-Finn

Founder/Managing Owner

Bright Start Early Care
& Preschool

Washington, DC

How long have you been in the child care industry?
17 years

What is your favorite hobby?
Traveling

Why do you love working in our industry?
The beauty of seeing the transformation of children into socially adapted communities.

How do you keep a positive mindset at work?
Sing/Listen to inspirational/motivational talks

What is your favorite PMA (Positive Mental Attitude) book?
The Slight Edge by Jeff Olson

When you are stressed at work, how do you de-stress?
I play inspirational music.

What do you do for fun when not working?

Spend time with family cooking, dancing, and debating world events.

Favorite Positive Quote:

"Stick to the fight when you're hardest hit - It's when things seem worst that you must not quit". ~ John Greenleaf Whittier

How has a positive mindset helped you with your career?

Makes me feel like I can do anything, empowered, nothing stands in my way. If I can think of it, I can achieve it.

How has a positive mindset helped you with life in general?

Positive mindset has allowed me to look at my challenges in life in a positive light. My challenges are seen as a launching pad to achieve my goals rather than a detour.

Samantha Phillips

Child Care Insurance
Specialist

Aleaf Insurance Agency

Frisco, TX

How long have you been in the child care industry?
Almost 8 Years

What is your favorite hobby?
Connecting – I love meeting new people, hearing their stories, and becoming friends. You can never have too many positive influences in your life!

Why do you love working in our industry?
I'm passionate about helping people, but it's a bonus helping people that are passionate about serving others! I get great joy in partnering with owners that I see give of themselves so selflessly to make their educational program the best it can be. It warms my heart!

How do you keep a positive mindset at work?
I don't view what I do as work but as an opportunity to serve. Colossians 3:23 is embedded in me. "Whatever you do, work at it with all your heart, as working for the Lord." When I sit down at my desk each day, I'm provided with numerous opportunities to make a positive impact on others. That excites me! Even when I was working under less than favorable circumstances, and that toxic environment had a negative

impact on my physical health and well-being, it never affected my quality of work! This verse and the positive mindset that comes with embracing a service first mentality is not something I preach. It is who I am.

What is your favorite PMA (Positive Mental Attitude) book?
The Bible for its consistent inspirational impact on my life.

When you are stressed at work, how do you de-stress?
I usually de-stress by getting up and doing something completely unrelated to work. I might say a little prayer, call a goofy friend that can always make me laugh, take a walk outside, or just get up and move for a few minutes, try a deep breathing or counting exercise, stretch on the ground, or something extremely random. For instance, I recently did a handstand just to see if I could. I recorded my goofy adventure and posted it on Facebook for others to laugh and enjoy. It immediately relieved my mind and helped me to feel like I had accomplished this big feat! How long has it been since you could say you've done a handstand? I felt awesome and very proud of myself ... even if the wall was holding me up! It's alright to do things outside of our comfort zone, and it's ok to laugh at yourself while doing it.

Favorite Positive Quote:
"If serving is beneath you, leadership is beyond you." ~ Anonymous

How has a positive mindset helped you with your career?
A positive mindset is very contagious in the sense that like-minded people are inevitably drawn to you. In my career, having a positive outlook and overall way of thinking has helped me attract similar clients and referral partners. These are people that I enjoy doing business with as much as they claim to enjoy doing business with me. Since positively-minded individuals attract other positively-minded individuals, my awesome clients are constantly referring me to their friends who are just as wonderful. Every person I take care of is amazing, and I consider them friends!

Joy Clore Willis

Owner

A Kids Gym Learning
Academy

Oviedo, FL

How long have you been in the child care Industry?
20+ Years

Why do you love working in our industry?
Seeing children learn and be happy.

How do you keep a positive mindset at work?
I truly love and care for people, children, and families.

What is your favorite PMA (Positive Mental Attitude) book?
"Start with Why" ~ Simon Sinek

When you are stressed at work, how do you de-stress?
I usually go for a run, not like running, more like an errand run, haha.

What do you do for fun when not working?
Horseback riding, camping and/or RVing. I Like to go to the beach and hike park trails.

Favorite Positive Quote:

"I get knocked down, but I get up again... I will survive." - Stephanie Bentley

What advice would you give for a new teacher on the importance of having a positive mindset?

Each day is a precious gift. We have to make a difference in these children's lives, they will remember us by how they are treated. Love them well...

How has a positive mindset helped you with your career?

I'm understanding more of the people side and I love to teach, so children and adults alike are set to be learners.

How has a positive mindset helped you with life in general?

When I was in my youth it helped me because I was super outgoing and would talk to anyone, anywhere. I'm generally a happy positive person to be around.

Steve Lloyd

Owner

Busy Little Hands Early
Learning Center

Centennial, CO

How long have you been in the child care industry?
10+ years

What is your favorite hobby?
Hiking

Why do you love working in our industry?
We are preparing children for an unknown future world. It is very fulfilling to help sculpt them into the person they will be for the rest of their lives. Children are the future.

How do you keep a positive mindset at work?
I remind myself why the work we do really does matter. When you understand your WHY, it will motivate you through good times and bad.

What is your favorite PMA (Positive Mental Attitude) book?
The Slight Edge – Jeff Olson. When this book is taken seriously, it can change your mindset forever.

When you are stressed at work, how do you de-stress?

I work out, meet my wife for lunch, or leave the school for a few minutes and go for a walk.

What do you do for fun when not working?

Travel, Camping, Hiking, or video games.

Who is the one person you admire the most? Why?

Jesus Christ. He is the person I strive to be like every day.

What advice would you give to someone just starting out in the childcare industry?

Define your WHY and your MISSION and you can do anything.

Favorite Positive Quote:

"God left the world unfinished for man to work his skill upon. He left the electricity in the cloud, the oil in the earth. He left the rivers unbridged and the cities unbuilt. God gives us the challenge of raw materials, not the ease of finished things. He leaves the pictures unpainted and the music unsung and the problems unsolved, that we might know the joys and glories of creation." ~Thomas S. Monson

What advice would you give for a new teacher on the importance of having a positive mindset?

Mindset is the first step to a happy life. Belief is the first ingredient to success.

How has a positive mindset helped you with your career?

With a positive mindset, I have reached almost every goal I have set for myself and my dreams seem tangible and within reach.

How has a positive mindset helped you with life in general?

With a positive mindset, I realized in order to be my BEST self I need to take care of myself. As a leader, we take care of the needs of others before ourselves and I realized I need to take care of my needs so I can be the best for everyone else. My health has improved, my relationships are stronger, and I am more focused and committed to taking care of my people.

Kathy Cameron

Owner

Guiding Hands Christian
Academy

Collinsville, TX

How long have you been in the child care industry?
12 years

Why do you love working in our industry?
I love teaching children and helping parents.

How do you keep a positive mindset at work?
I love what I do and I truly enjoy my life.

When you are stressed at work, how do you de-stress?
I work on the problem at hand.

What do you do for fun when not working?
Ride my horse, Dot, and spend time with my family.

Who is the one person you admire the most? Why?
My husband, Jered: he is the hardest working and most humble person I know.

What advice would you give to someone just starting out in the child care industry?

Get as much training in the areas you struggle in as you can. Leave the ugly at work, try not to bring it home.

Favorite Positive Quote:

"I can do all things through Christ, who strengthens me". Phil 4:13 NKJV

What advice would you give for a new teacher on the importance of having a positive mindset?

The teacher sets the tone for the entire class. If you want to have a fantastic day, be in a fun, compassionate mood.

Have you always had a positive mindset from childhood or did you develop it as an adult?

I have always had a positive mindset due to my upbringing. My mom is a very positive person. She is always smiling.

How has a positive mindset helped you with your career?

When times are difficult, I try to remind myself that if I get stuck in my upset, I'll never get past it.

Sindye Alexander

Director of Marketing

Owned: Munchkin Manor
University

Petoskey, MI

I owned Munchkin Manor University from 2011 to 2016, after I sold my center I joined Kris's team with the Child Care Success Company.

How long have you been in the child care industry?

24+ years

What is your favorite PMA (Positive Mental Attitude) book?

Leaders Eat Last by Simon Sinek

When you are stressed at work, how do you de-stress?

First, I try some deep breathing exercises and turn to books or podcasts to help bring me out of my funk. I try to pour more positive messages into my soul to drive out the negativity that is trying to set up camp in my mind. I am a fairly private person, and don't like to share that I am struggling unless I absolutely have to. I tend to feel like I need to be strong and figure it out on my own. So, I try to do that first.

What advice would you give to someone just starting out in the childcare industry?

To an owner or director, I would say, "Don't try to do this alone!" Find yourself a group of safe peers that you can bounce ideas off of, ask advice of, and just be friends with. The group I would recommend would be the Child Care Success Academy, but if you don't feel that one is right for you, find one that is. You need people that will be there to support you and talk you through some of the toughest situations you will face. Also, it is important to hire people that are better than you at the things you're not so good at. It's OKAY to know you are not good at everything, and to hire people who can offset your weaknesses. I wish I would have done this sooner in my own business.

To teachers and caregivers, I would remind them of the direct impact they are making on the lives of these children every single day. Every interaction and caring gesture is building their little brains and establishing patterns for future learning. What you do might not seem glamorous in the "day-in, day-out" parts of the job. However, if you can remember the impact you are making long term, it can help you stay positive and fulfilled in your work. I'd also advise participating in as much professional development as possible. You should be working to continually develop yourself and your skills. I remember thinking one time early on in my career that "all these continuing ed hours that licensing requires is so stupid." You see, I thought I knew everything I need to know. But what happened was, the more training and education I received, the more I realized there was SO MUCH I didn't know! The more new techniques and theories I learned, the better teacher I became. Never stop learning or developing yourself!

Favorite Positive Quote:
There are SO MANY!! I love collecting positive quotes. It is really hard to narrow it down.

"The primary ingredient for progress is optimism. The unwavering belief that something can be better is what drives us forward." – Simon Sinek

How has a positive mindset helped you with your career?
Keeping a positive mindset has helped me to accomplish many of the big goals that I've had for myself. Some things seem impossible. But when I made a decision or a commitment toward accomplishing a goal, and then stayed positive even in the face of hurdles and roadblocks that would pop up along the way, I always found a way to accomplish my vision/goal. It's like the act of committing to accomplishing a particular goal almost invites the universe to orchestrate "things" to come together on your behalf. Your mindset is key in manifesting what you need to get you to your big goals.

Hemang Patel

Owner

Kiddie Academy of
Ellicott City
Columbia
Laurel

Ellicott City, MD

How long have you been in the child care industry?
Started this journey in 2015.

Why do you love working in our industry?
Teaching is in my blood. I have grown up around teachers, my dad's side of the family is full of teachers. I think "this was my calling" and I picked this field subconsciously. I love this field because I am making a positive impact with students and teachers. Business comes naturally to me so it gets a little easier. I can easily connect with children. I can solve problems.

How do you keep a positive mindset at work?
Constantly reminding myself that I am doing this for service over anything else. A challenging situation does affect me, but my goal in life is to convert that negative emotion into positive as soon as possible.

What is your favorite PMA (Positive Mental Attitude) book?
I prefer listening, as it is faster than reading. I listen to Brahma Kumari Sister Shivani speeches; her wisdom puts things into perspective quickly. I was lucky enough to meet her personally as well.

What advice would you give to someone just starting out in the childcare industry?

Make sure you know why you are doing this. I have done many challenging things in life and worked in many industries; the child care industry is a challenging field. Make sure you know why you are doing it and you are clear about your expectations from this field.

What advice would you give for a new teacher on the importance of having a positive mindset?

Be prepared for next week with activities, materials, and mindset. Focus on customer service and classroom execution. There are many distractions and if you involve yourself with distractions, you will NOT be living your purpose successfully as a teacher and as a human being.

How has a positive mindset helped you with your career?

Life is energy, everything around you is energy. You decide what kind of energy you want to have, Positive and negative. Positive energy attracts positive people and positive things, negative energy attracts negative people and negative things.

Jaime Moran

Owner

Over the Rainbow of
Cheshire
Hamden

Cheshire, CT

How long have you been in the child care industry?
I purchased my first center in 2012, prior to that I was a kindergarten teacher.

Why do you love working in our industry?
This industry can be an exhausting job, and most people don't give enough credit to child care providers. But, the minute I walk through the door and I am greeted by all the kids running to give me a hug makes everything worth it. There is something about a hug from a child that makes the day worthwhile. Seeing the smile on their face, the fun they are having at school, and the joy after they complete a project or learn a new concept, puts everything into perspective. At the end of the day we are making a difference and guiding their path to be lifelong learners.

How do you keep a positive mindset at work?
Having support from my family helps me get through the day and knowing that I have an amazing team. Without my amazing directors and teachers, Over the Rainbow couldn't be possible.

What is your favorite PMA (Positive Mental Attitude) book?

The first positive book that I have read, The Slight Edge by Jeff Olson. This book was the first of many that have guided my path of a positive mindset.

When you are stressed at work, how do you de-stress?

Talking through an issue helps me.

What advice would you give to someone just starting out in the childcare industry?

Having a positive mindset is key to having a successful business. The way you view and react to situations will help shape the outcome and will pave a clear path to your vision.

Favorite Positive Quote:

"Count your rainbows, not your thunderstorms" ~ Alyssa Knight

What advice would you give for a new teacher on the importance of having a positive mindset?

Having a positive mindset trickles down to your students.

How has a positive mindset helped you with life in general?

Viewing things differently has helped me make different decisions that I normally wouldn't have made in life. I am always trying to look at the good of something that is happening rather than the bad.

Dalis Marie Ramos

Enrollment Specialist/
Director

Bells Ferry Learning Center

Woodstock, GA

How long have you been in the child care industry?

12 Years

What is your favorite hobby?

I love to cook International Food

Why do you love working in our industry?

I love to work in the child care industry because I know that I'm making a real difference in the lives of children and families.

How do you keep a positive mindset at work?

I surround myself with positivity every morning before walking through the door.

What is your favorite PMA (Positive Mental Attitude) book?

The PMA Effect by John Joseph

When you are stressed at work, how do you de-stress?

I schedule 10 minutes of "no worry time" for breathing exercises to inhale peace and positivity and exhale worries and negativity.

What advice would you give to someone just starting out in the childcare industry?

Be patient. Be positive. I promise this is one of the most rewarding jobs on the planet. We are building the future.

Favorite Positive Quote:

"People who are crazy enough to think they can change the world are the ones who do." ~ Rob Sittanen

What advice would you give for a new teacher on the importance of having a positive mindset?

Being positive is the key to your inner peace and to making an impact on the lives of children.

How has a positive mindset helped you with life in general?

I believe that a positive mindset has helped me block the fear of taking risks and going beyond boundaries in life.

Sara Schreiner

President - Owner

The Sunshine Academy

Laurel, MT

How long have you been in the child care industry?
18 years

What is your favorite hobby?
Camping and cooking

Why do you love working in our industry?
The work we do matters: it changes the world.

How do you keep a positive mindset at work?
I keep a positive mindset by setting and enforcing boundaries which promote and encourage it. I am intentional about finding the good and share it when I see it. I practice gratitude daily, even on the difficult days. Finally, when there are any issues which conflict with my core values, I address them quickly, clearly, and kindly rather than dwelling on them.

What is your favorite PMA (Positive Mental Attitude) book?
Girl Wash Your Face by Rachel Hollis

When you are stressed at work, how do you de-stress?

My family keeps me grounded and time with them is by far the best way to de-stress. My husband knows me better than anyone. I have learned to trust his judgment; he picks up on my stress and tells me it is time to refocus and regain perspective. I also practice gratitude and prayer daily.

Who is the one person you admire the most? Why?

I most admire my brother, Keith. As a child he was injured in a fluke medical accident, leaving him with chronic pain. Rather than focusing on the tragic circumstances, he has chosen to make a good and successful life. He is a generous man and always available to help others, regardless of the personal or physical cost he may pay. Keith taught me that mindset has absolutely nothing to do with the circumstances surrounding you and everything to do with the life you choose to live in spite of them.

What advice would you give to someone just starting out in the childcare industry?

Keep your eyes on the big picture. It is easy to become distracted by the small daily irritants and issues which will arise. Shifting your focus to the lasting impact you and your program will have on students, families, and the community will help you achieve greatness.

Favorite Positive Quote:

"We must embrace the belief that each person is uniquely prepared, eager to learn and full of potential if we are to make a difference in their life."
~ Sara Schreiner

What advice would you give for a new teacher on the importance of having a positive mindset?

There will be students who drive you bonkers, parents who continually question you and coworkers who are in the industry for all of the wrong reasons. Each of these things has the potential to prevent you from making the difference you were put on this earth to make. A positive mindset is your greatest weapon in defeating these obstacles.

How has a positive mindset helped you with life in general?

It has made the hard days more bearable and the good days even brighter. I now have the courage and confidence to persevere and conquer new challenges. I believe it has made me a better, stronger leader as this mindset supports a commitment to growth, encouragement, and excellence.